# THE HARDER THEY FALL

*by*

DeVon White

**Prosperity Publishing Solutions Est: 2025**

www.prosperitypublishing.net

Other novels by DeVon White

I Can See Clearly Now

The Prodigal Son

**Release Oct 2025:** The Sword (Honoring The Code)

The Harder They Fall

Author: DeVon White

Copyright © 2025 Prosperity Publishing Solutions.

All rights reserved, including the right of reproduction in whole or in part in any form.

Edition: First Prosperity Publishing Solutions Edition

Purchase copies: *The Harder They Fall*:
Available online: Amazon, Barnes & Noble, IngramSpark, and D2D

The Harder They Fall is a powerful tale of quiet resilience, self-discovery, and earned triumph. Taylor Wilson, once a quiet girl silenced by bullying and grief, finds solace in books and cappuccinos. Love introduces her to a world of privilege that soon turns cruel.

When Jaren Best, heir to a powerful empire, fails to defend her, Taylor is forced to confront not only betrayal but the legacy of silence that has surrounded her life. What begins as heartbreak becomes transformation. Armed with her father's wisdom and a journal of hidden truths, she uncovers the corruption behind the Best name and rises, not in anger, but in grace.

Through heartbreak, exposure, and fierce self-possession, Taylor reclaims her voice. She does not shatter the world. She rewrites it.

This is not just a story of falling. It is a story of rising. Of becoming. Of a woman who learns that quiet can be power, and that the softest voice can change everything.

**DeVon White**

## Dedication

For my daughters, who teach me every day what strength looks like. For my wife, whose grace has shaped the man I am. For my mother and sisters, who carried dreams in silence so I could find my voice.

And for every woman whose courage changed the room.

This story is yours.

---

## Author's Note

As a son, a husband, a father, and a brother, I have spent my life watching the quiet power of women, how they build, endure, and rise with little recognition.

This novel is a tribute to that strength. Taylor's journey was born from my hope that my daughters always know their voices matter, their softness is strength, and their dreams have no ceilings.

Though fictional, this story holds truth in every corner. It was written with reverence and love. If it resonates, it is because the women in our lives have already lived its pages.

Thank you for reading.

**DeVon White**

# Table of Contents

## ACT I: The Breaking and the Becoming

1. The Weight of Books
2. Fathers and Ghosts
3. Wings in a Teacup
4. The Cappuccino Mirror
5. Gentle Breezes, Poetic Sunrises
6. Fabric of a Dream

## ACT II: The Cracks in Porcelain

7. Silhouettes in the Foam
8. Gold Dust and Razor Words
9. The Echo of Her Name
10. Dissonance in D Minor
11. Lamb Among Lions
12. Keys to Secrets

## ACT III: The Awakening

13. Stillness at the Door
14. Lessons from a Narcissist
15. Operation Payback
16. The Boutique of Becoming
17. Sleeping with Serpents
18. Lockpicks and Lineage

## ACT IV: The Fall

19. The Silent Stake

20. The Gentle Revolution
21. Cappuccino Queen
22. Echoes from the Past
23. The Auction of Empires
24. The Harder They Fall

---

**Epilogue**
Porcelain Wings

*The Harder They Fall*

## Chapter 1: The Weight of Books

The walk home from school was always the longest part of Taylor Wilson's day.

Not because the distance was insurmountable, or the sidewalks particularly arduous. Rather, it was the silence that accompanied each step, a quietude that cloaked her in a sense of isolation. Her backpack, a hand-me-down far too large for her frame, seemed to grow heavier with each passing moment, laden with textbooks and notebooks that offered far more comfort than the company of her peers. Her algebra book was bound together with a rubber band, its spine long since surrendered to wear, but Taylor valued it, nonetheless. Numbers were consistent. Words, even more so. They did not turn against you.

The route she traveled was familiar, etched in muscle memory. And yet, every afternoon, it felt foreign, as though her existence along that path was tolerated rather than embraced. She kept her head bowed, eyes cast downward, shoulders tucked in, as if to render herself invisible.

Behind her, laughter sliced through the air.

"Taylor-Timid."

The nickname, cruel, childish, and undeserved, had taken root. It followed her through the corridors and into the daylight, whispered with amused contempt by those who thrived on hierarchy.

"I imagine she organizes her bookshelf alphabetically and color-coded," one voice remarked with mock sophistication, followed by a chorus of insincere laughter.

Taylor chose not to respond. Retorts only invited escalation. Her silence was not born of defeat but of careful calculation. It was the quiet dignity of someone who had long since decided that their worth would not be debated by those incapable of understanding it.

By the time she reached the modest home she shared with her mother, the scent of dinner, drifted through the open window. It was the kind of smell that evoked comfort and nostalgia, a symphony that reminded her she was, at the very least, cherished within these walls.

The porch welcomed her with a creak, the screen door screeching slightly as she stepped inside.

"Is that you, Taylor?" her mother's voice called, warm and reassuring.

"Yes, Mother," she replied.

"Dinner is nearly ready. How are you?"

Taylor hesitated. She could have explained the events of the day, the laughter, the mockery, the fatigue that weighed heavier than her bag. But she knew her mother's heart already bore too much.

"I am. Just a bit weary," she said softly.

Her mother emerged from the kitchen, apron tied neatly around her waist, hands slightly flour-dusted. She took one look at Taylor and said nothing. Instead, she approached and gently cupped her daughter's face, brushing her cheeks with quiet affection.

"Go freshen up. I'll prepare your plate."

Taylor offered a faint smile before ascending the stairs to her room. There, she unzipped her backpack and laid its contents across the bed: textbooks, notepads, and a journal adorned with pressed violets and a satin ribbon.

She opened it to a fresh page.

"Today, I faded into the background once more. The sting lessens with each occurrence. Perhaps I am becoming adept at being unseen, invisible."

She closed the journal and held it close to her chest. Outside, the setting sun painted its silhouette on the walls. Taylor sat on the edge of her bed, allowing herself to remember.

Her father.

His voice was her earliest lullaby, a soothing baritone that read her everything from encyclopedias to poetry. He believed knowledge was not only power but refuge.

*"Words are like constellations, Taybird," "Even when the night is darkest, they can guide you home."*

She remembered his laughter, warm and infectious, and the gentle way he used to place notes in her lunchbox, each inscribed with a phrase of encouragement. She had kept every one. They were her private inheritance.

Then came the day he collapsed, suddenly, silently. The hospital offered no real answers. But Taylor knew. It was heartbreak that claimed him. After her two elder brothers were lost to the war, something inside of him had withered.

Grief became the nightmarish houseguest that didn't knock; it just entered without invitation and never departed. It settled in the corners of rooms and in hidden spaces.

She reached for her English book, pressing her fragile face against the worn cover. A tear, then another, then another slid down her cheek, being absorbed by the pages of the book nestled to her cheek. As if finding comfort without feeling the emotion of guilt.

She would not shatter. Not now. Not yet.

She turned off the lamp and drew the covers up to her chin. In the darkness, she whispered, "You are not invisible. You are not irrelevant."

And for the briefest moment, she believed it.

Sleep came gently, and with it, a dream.

Her father stood at the end of her bed, his eyes kind, hands tucked into the pockets of his favorite cardigan.

"Still bearing the weight of the world, Taybird?" he asked, voice tender.

She nodded, overwhelmed.

He approached and kissed her forehead. "You are stronger than your sorrow. And one day, the world will see you as I do."

The next morning, she rose before the sun, methodically dressing in her school uniform. She tied her hair with the blue ribbon her aunt had given her last Christmas and stood in front of the mirror. The reflection that met her eyes was quiet, but no longer tentative.

She opened her journal once more and wrote:

"This will be the last day I allow the voices of others to weigh me down like an anchor. This day, I shall carry only my own banner. Be my own light. Discover me."

With that, she slipped her arms through the straps of her worn backpack. It was still heavy, but now, it felt like purpose.

## Chapter 2: Fathers and Ghosts

The morning sun filtered through the linen curtains, casting patterns of gold across Taylor Wilson's bedroom floor. The world outside stirred gently, birds in chorus, wind brushing the branches in whispering gestures, and the occasional hum of a neighbor's engine starting down the block. But within the confines of her room, time held stillness like breath before a sigh.

Taylor sat at her desk, a slender figure cloaked in introspection. She had not slept well. Dreams, though tender in tone, had stirred memories best left undisturbed. Her father's face had returned to her in the night, gentle, solemn, full of unspoken understanding.

She opened the drawer of her writing desk and retrieved an envelope, yellowing at the edges but unwrinkled, preserved with almost sacred care. Inside was one of his many letters. Her father had left her a note every week for years, small affirmations folded with precision and tucked into the corners of her world, between the pages of her books, into the sleeves of her sweaters, under her pillow. She read this one slowly, aloud but barely above a whisper:

*"Taybird, your light is quiet, but it reaches further than you know. Remember to let no one dim it. Love, Dad."*

A tremor passed through her, subtle but resolute. She pressed the note to her heart, then placed it back in its envelope. Memories of him rarely arrived without a cost.

They brought warmth, yes, but also an ache that found shelter in her heart, where it nestled like something permanent.

She rose and crossed the room to the window. The view offered little change, rooftops softened by dew, sidewalks still damp from last night's rain, but today it felt more distant. She longed, suddenly and acutely, for the comfort of her father's study. Though it had been left largely untouched since his passing, it remained a sanctuary, as though the walls had memorized the rhythm of his presence.

Descending the staircase quietly, she moved through the hallway, her fingertips grazing the pictures mounted along the wall: a younger version of herself grinning with gap-toothed delight; her two brothers, posed in uniform, forever youthful in the captured stillness of time; and in the center, her father, book in hand, eyes crinkled with a smile.

The door to the study opened with a familiar creak. Dust particles danced in the morning light, swirling in lazy spirals. The lingering scent of her father met her like a welcome embrace. The desk, still adorned with his reading glasses and an unopened fountain pen, bore the weight of history.

She approached the shelves slowly, letting her fingers trace the bindings of old volumes. There was the poetry of Yeats, the biographies of great philosophers, his annotated edition of James Baldwin. Her father had once told her that strength was born not of dominance, but of stillness.

"He who commands himself," he would say, "needs no crown to be a king."

Taylor sank into the leather armchair, one far too large for her when she was younger, but now it felt as though it had waited for her. She closed her eyes and, for a moment, allowed herself to believe he was near.

"Dad," she murmured. "I wish you could see me now. I'm trying so hard to be what you believed I could be."

Tears began to rise, but Taylor did not allow them to fall. There was a grace in that restraint, a lesson her father had modeled many times over. She remembered the way he grieved for her brothers: silently, with hands that shook only when he thought no one was watching. And yet, he had never lost his capacity for kindness, for love, for compassion, even under the burden of immeasurable loss.

Her mother's footsteps padded softly down the hallway. Taylor heard her pause outside the door.

"You're in there, aren't you?" her mother said gently.

"Yes."

"Breakfast is ready. Take your time."

"Thank you, Mother."

There was love in her mother's voice, though it was tinged with a sorrow she rarely gave name to. They had all lost so much. The difference, Taylor often thought, was that her mother wore her grief with dignity, while Taylor still struggled to tailor hers.

Before she left the room, Taylor took a small book of quotations from the shelf, one she and her father used to read from together, and slipped it into her satchel. A sword of words, perhaps, for the mental battles of the day.

Later, as she sat at the kitchen table, her mother served breakfast without ceremony. Slices of buttered toast, eggs scrambled to perfection, and a bowl of sliced apples.

"You were quiet last night," her mother said after a long pause.

"I was remembering."

Her mother nodded. "I think about him every day."

"I know."

A silence settled between them, not heavy but of honoring his memory.

"He'd be proud of you, Taylor."

The words struck with more weight than she expected. She bowed her head slightly, eyes fixed on her plate.

"I hope so."

Her mother reached across the table and placed her hand gently over Taylor's.

"He always said you were his compass."

Taylor looked up, eyes wide with surprise. "He never told me that."

"He didn't have to," her mother said, smiling faintly. "He showed it every day."

For the remainder of the meal, they ate quietly, the kind of silence that speaks in volumes.

And when Taylor left for school that morning, she walked with her head slightly higher. Not because the world had changed, but because she carried with her the memory of a man who saw her not as she was, but as she could be.

A quiet legacy. A silent strength. A father's ghost, and the light he left behind.

---

**Chapter 3: Wings in a Teacup**

The city hummed with its usual symphony of polished chaos, horns honking in soft rhythm, footsteps clicking along concrete like metronomes of urgency, and the faint melody of street musicians. But within the walls of the uptown café, there was a stillness that defied the bustle outside.

Taylor Wilson paused just before the entrance, inhaling deeply. Her breath rose in a quiet plume, mingling with the autumn chill. This place had become her sanctuary, her stage, and on days when the world refused to see her, the café granted her the dignity of being noticed, if only by the chandeliers and the baristas in their finely pressed suits.

She stepped inside, the gentle chime of the door announcing her arrival. The marble floor, smooth and elegant beneath her feet, reflected the cascading crystals of the light fixtures above. A cello played softly over hidden speakers.

Taylor made her way to the counter with graceful purpose. The barista, a man with silver-rimmed glasses and an unshakable professionalism, offered a cordial nod.

She took a breath, then delivered her now-ritualistic order with deliberate flair:

*"Ah, yes. I shall have a cappuccino masterpiece, not merely a drink, but a work of reverent artistry. I require*

*the finest, single-origin espresso, hand-selected from a micro-lot so exclusive it is spoken of in hushed reverence by connoisseurs. The milk must be of impeccable lineage, organic, of course, and gently frothed to a texture reminiscent of clouds on a spring morning. As for the foam, let it be sculpted with the delicacy of cherubs and crowned with a gold-dusted cocoa silhouette of Michelangelo's David. Or, should your hand be steady enough, perhaps my own profile. And do serve it in porcelain so delicate it might weep from the honor."*

The barista responded with a faint smile of admiration and began to work.

Taylor turned toward the seating area, selecting her favorite table near the window. The sunlight fell across it like a blessing. She arranged her satchel, removed her journal, and smoothed its spine with a sense of bravado and zeal. This weekly ritual had become more than a luxury, it was a declaration. In this café, she was not the quiet girl who blended into lockers and shadows. She was a woman of elegance, purpose, and wit. Here, she belonged.

The first time she had ordered her cappuccino in that now-famous cadence, it had been a joke, a secret rebellion against the grey weight of a particularly brutal week. But something had shifted the moment she spoke those words aloud. Heads had turned. Not in ridicule, but in intrigue. It was the first time she had chosen to speak herself into existence, into relevance, into being free, and in doing so, she was announcing to the world who the real Taylor Wilson is and who she was determined to be.

As she waited for her drink, she gazed out the window. Children clutched the hands of their parents, couples strolled by with their shoulders pressed together, and cyclists navigated through the crowd like silent messengers. She imagined each passerby with a story, a secret, a hope they kept in their mental care.

The barista approached with reverence, setting down her cappuccino with practiced grace.

"Your masterpiece, Miss."

Taylor nodded graciously. "And indeed, a masterpiece it is."

She lifted the porcelain cup, admiring the delicate curve of the handle and the precise pattern of cocoa atop the foam. She took a sip. It was divine.

Closing her eyes for a moment, she allowed herself to simply be. Not to perform, not to defend, but to exist without explanation.

Her journal lay open before her, and she began to write.

"Today, I tasted joy disguised as cappuccino. It lingered, gently, like a memory that hasn't yet decided whether to make you smile or weep. This moment, brief and beautiful, is mine."

She was so immersed in the act of capturing her thoughts that she did not notice the man who had stepped into line behind her minutes earlier, nor the way he watched her with amused curiosity as she spoke her elaborate order. He, too, ordered the very same drink, with the very same dramatic cadence, his voice rich with irony and something else, interest.

Jaren Best III was not a man accustomed to curiosity. Most things in his world were known, categorized, and within his control. But there was something about the woman seated by the window, sipping her cappuccino as if it were a declaration of sovereignty, that unsettled him, in the most delightful way.

He approached slowly, cappuccino in hand, and as he passed her table, he offered a nod.

"Forgive the intrusion, but I must say, your soliloquy at the counter was nothing short of legendary."

Taylor looked up, startled but composed.

"You've heard it before?"

He grinned. "No, but I've rehearsed one of my own."

She raised an eyebrow. "You've plagiarized my moment."

"Improvised, surely."

Taylor smiled, faintly, but genuinely.

"Well, then," she replied, gesturing to the seat across from her, "join me. Let us toast to fleeting theatrics and perfectly frothed milk."

Jaren accepted the invitation with the ease of someone who never, heard 'no,' yet in this moment, he knew it was not an assumption, but a gift.

Their conversation began with cappuccinos and theatrics, but soon unraveled into the architecture of language, the politics of silence, and the quiet art of observation. Taylor surprised herself. She was never this open, this fluid with strangers. But Jaren, for all his charm and polished affect, seemed intrigued not by what she could offer him, but by who she was when unguarded.

And so, in a café gilded with chandeliers and perfumed with espresso, two lives briefly intersected. Neither knew what would follow, but both left with the taste of something rare.

For Taylor, it was the first time someone had noticed not just her presence, but her essence.

For Jaren, it was the first time a woman had not bent beneath the weight of his charisma.

In their shared laughter, amid curls of steam rising from twin porcelain cups, something delicate took root.

Wings, folded and waiting, in a teacup.

## Chapter 4: The Cappuccino Mirror

The following week arrived draped in a golden haze, autumn sunlight filtering through Manhattan's canopy of amber and leaves. Taylor Wilson adjusted the scarf around her neck, a soft cashmere gift she had once bought for herself on a particularly difficult day. As she approached the familiar glass doors of the café, she carried with her a renewed sense of anticipation. She hadn't expected to look forward to this moment, hadn't expected a stranger to linger in her thoughts. Yet, there it was: the recollection of a man with a tailored voice and a mischievous smile who had shared her table, her drink, and a corner of her world.

She stepped inside, and the ambiance welcomed her like an old friend. The soft melody playing in the background, the gentle clink of porcelain, and the warm aroma of roasted beans stirred something nostalgic and comforting. As she approached the counter, she smoothed her coat, tucked a strand of hair behind her ear, and readied her now-rehearsed lines.

But before she could speak, a voice just behind her spoke with amused precision:

"Ah, yes, I shall have a cappuccino masterpiece, not merely a drink, but an experience worthy of verse."

Taylor turned slowly, already recognizing the familiar cadence.

Jaren Best III stood there, sharply dressed yet relaxed, his eyes gleaming with a mischievous charm. He completed the full theatrical order, nearly word for word, and bowed subtly as the barista nodded in dry amusement.

Taylor raised an eyebrow. "You've memorized it."

"Of course. One doesn't forget a performance that captivating," he replied smoothly.

"I wasn't performing."

"Then I am doubly impressed."

The two stood side by side, awaiting their orders, trying not to appear too aware of one another's presence. Their eyes met in the polished reflection of the marble countertop, a mirrored glance that carried a spark of interest and something softer, more uncertain.

"So," Taylor said, turning slightly toward him. "Do you make a habit of following strangers into cafés?"

"Only the exceptional ones."

Taylor found herself smiling, though she didn't offer it freely. It emerged despite her, and it lingered longer than she intended.

They took their drinks and returned to the same table near the window. Taylor's journal remained closed this time. She felt strangely exposed, not in a vulnerable way, but as if her thoughts might already be read without ink or pages.

"Jaren," he said, extending a hand with gentle formality.

"Taylor," she replied, her grip steady, her name sounding somehow more certain on his lips.

"So, Taylor," he began as he settled into the chair, "what inspires such vivid coffee orders?"

She looked down at her cup, then back at him. "There's power in imagination. In taking something ordinary and making it extraordinary, even for just a moment. I suppose it's my way of stepping into a different life. One where I am... more."

He nodded, watching her intently. "And what's wrong with the life you already have?"

She hesitated. "Nothing, on the surface. But not all wounds are visible."

A pause passed between them. The café around them blurred into the background.

"You're very composed," Jaren observed. "But I suspect you weren't always."

Taylor's smile faltered slightly. "There was a time when I wasn't anyone. Or at least, not anyone people saw."

He waited, respectful of her pace.

"In school," she said quietly, "I was the girl they ignored. Or worse, the one they remembered only when they needed someone to mock. I used to believe I was invisible, and that being invisible was safer. But invisibility is a slow erasure. Eventually, you forget you were ever whole."

Jaren didn't interrupt. He simply looked at her, not with pity, but with a curiosity that felt strangely gentle.

"I'm not that girl anymore," Taylor added. "This", she lifted her cup slightly, "is my armor."

"I think it's more than that," Jaren said. "It's your banner."

She tilted her head. "You speak like someone who's observed battles from the inside."

"Perhaps," he replied. "Or perhaps I just recognize the bravery in choosing joy, however briefly."

They continued speaking, about books and cities, about the poetry of silence and the brutality of ambition. Taylor learned that Jaren had studied in Oxford, that he spoke several languages, and that he came from a world both glamorous and relentless. He learned that she had grown up in modest means, that she had once dreamed of becoming a literature professor, and that her favorite poem was Dickinson's "Hope is the thing with feathers."

"Hope," Jaren repeated, softly. "Do you still believe in it?"

"I have to," Taylor said. "Because it's what gets me from one cappuccino to the next."

He laughed at that, and so did she.

When they finally stood to leave, the afternoon sun had begun its descent. Outside, the city was still moving, but within them, something had paused, settled.

"I'd like to see you again," Jaren said, adjusting the collar of his coat.

Taylor considered him for a long moment, then reached for her journal.

She tore a page neatly from the back, scribbled something, and handed it to him.

"A time. A place. If you're sincere."

Their fingers brushed as he accepted it. He nodded. "Sincerity isn't always my strong suit. But for this, I'll make an exception."

As Taylor stepped away, she glanced once at the mirror above the counter. For the first time, her reflection didn't seem like a stranger.

It looked like a woman standing on the threshold of something remarkable.

## Chapter 5: Gentle Breezes, Poetic Sunrises

It began subtly, like a waltz barely audible through an open window, this shift in Taylor's life. As if someone had reached into her story and changed the tempo. What had started as a shared cup of cappuccino evolved into moments exchanged between quiet hearts. With Jaren Best III, time felt less jagged. Their conversations meandered through the intricate pathways of literature, philosophy, and dreams, both fulfilled and forgotten.

Taylor had grown accustomed to solitude, not the barren kind, but the kind that allowed her thoughts room to stretch, to unfurl like ribbons in a breeze. But now, someone was there to share in the fruit of her thoughts, not as an intrusion but as a welcome guest.

Their meetings became more frequent, yet never contrived. They strolled through Central Park beneath trees, and the golden hues of October shone upon them. They wandered through bookstores, where Jaren marveled at Taylor's ability to recall obscure authors and first editions. They dined at small cafés tucked in corners of the city that Jaren had never noticed before. With Taylor, he found simplicity profound.

One morning, Jaren invited Taylor to visit his family's estate in the Hudson Valley, a place, he said, "where the earth still remembers what elegance once felt like."

She hesitated. Though intrigued by his world, she feared becoming a guest in a life she could not inhabit. But something in his tone, a softness, rare and unguarded, persuaded her.

The estate greeted her with open arms and ancient trees. The gravel path whispered beneath their steps as they walked side by side, the silence between them comfortable and golden. The Best family's ancestral home stood like a painting come to life, grand, yes, but softened by ivy and time.

"This place," Jaren said as they stepped onto the terrace, "has seen centuries of ambition and pride. And yet, mornings here are always the same, humble, honest."

Taylor turned her face to the breeze. The wind here did not rush. It lingered.

They sat overlooking a hillside blanketed in wildflowers. A servant arrived with two delicate china cups and a pot of tea. Taylor took hers gratefully, hands warming around the porcelain.

"You're different here," she observed.

Jaren looked at her, expression unreadable. "Here, I don't have to be anything."

They sipped their tea in thoughtful silence. The morning stretched out around them like an unfinished poem.

"Do you believe," Taylor began slowly, "that people can change?"

Jaren considered this, then answered, "I believe people can be reminded of who they were before the world instructed them otherwise."

His gaze fell to her hands, delicate, composed, and resting gently on her lap.

"You ground me," he said, almost absently.

Taylor met his eyes. "Then perhaps I should leave you floating. There's a certain danger in needing what you can't define."

He smiled, but there was a note of sorrow in it. "Spoken like someone who's been hurt before."

Taylor looked away, to the horizon where sun and sky embraced with quiet reverence. "Hurt is a language I speak fluently."

"May I ask?" he said gently.

She shook her head. "Not today."

And he respected that.

Later, they wandered into the estate's private garden. Jaren pointed to a wrought iron bench beneath a white dogwood tree.

"My mother used to sit there for hours. Said the tree listened better than most people."

Taylor smiled. "Your mother sounds like someone I would like."

"She would like you," he replied, with a certainty that surprised even himself.

As the sun dipped lower, casting elongated shadows, Taylor stood in the soft light, her dress stirring in the wind like a whisper. She felt something unspoken pass between them, a tenderness not yet named. But it trembled in the space they shared.

That night, back in her apartment, Taylor could not sleep. She lay curled beneath her quilt, the scent of Jaren's cologne still faintly present in her scarf. She opened her journal and wrote:

"Today, the wind carried my name. It did not shout, but whispered, Taylor, you are seen. Not for the performance, but for the pauses. And in that pause, I found a sunrise inside myself."

She closed the journal and held it close, her thoughts a delicate balance between fear and wonder.

For the first time in years, she did not dream of the past.

She dreamed of tomorrow.

---

## Chapter 6: Fabric of a Dream

Taylor stood before the boutique window, her breath lightly fogging the glass. On the other side, a dress shimmered under the warm spotlights, champagne silk with a delicate overlay of ivory lace, the kind of dress that seemed to hum with possibility. It had been there for weeks, displayed like a promise she dared not claim. But today, something felt different.

Behind her, the city murmured its usual rhythm, but Taylor's world had shifted. She now moved through her days not as a shadow, but as someone awakening from a long, quiet slumber. Her meetings with Jaren had stirred her imagination and unsettled her doubts. The days of disappearing into corners had softened into a season of becoming. She was still cautious, still gentle, but no longer invisible.

Her fingers hovered above the door handle, then closed around it with quiet resolve. Inside, the boutique was hushed and fragrant with rosewater. A woman in a tailored black dress approached, offering a smile polished by years of refinement.

"May I help you?"

Taylor nodded. "I'd like to try on the dress in the window."

"Of course. Follow me."

Moments later, Taylor stood in the dressing room, the gown draped over her arm like a secret finally confessed. She slipped it on slowly and carefully, as though stepping into a memory she had never lived but somehow knew.

The mirror reflected a woman she did not fully recognize. The fabric kissed her shoulders, fell like liquid along her frame, and pooled at her feet like moonlight. She exhaled, a sound soft and tremulous.

It was not vanity that stirred her. It was something deeper, a validation, perhaps, that she could be someone worthy of notice. Someone who belonged in a room, not simply occupied it.

As she emerged from the dressing room, the attendant clasped her hands. "It looks as though it were made for you."

Taylor studied her reflection again. "I think," she said carefully, "I would like to purchase it."

Back home, she opened the tin box beneath her bed, where her savings lay wrapped in an old scarf. She counted the bills with the reverence of someone counting heartbeats. It would cost her more than she could easily afford, but this was not frivolity. This was living.

She laid the dress across her bed and stared at it, as if it might offer guidance. She could still hear Jaren's voice, the invitation he had extended so casually to attend his friend's party. He had mentioned it in passing, as though it were of little consequence. But Taylor had not taken it lightly.

This would be the first time she would meet the others, the ones who belonged to Jaren's world. A world defined by privilege and pedigree. She wondered what they would see when they looked at her.

Would they notice the carefully chosen pearls from her mother's jewelry box? Would they recognize the courage it took to walk into a room built for someone else and stand with unshaken grace?

Taylor smoothed the gown, then placed it back in its protective covering. She was no longer the girl who ran home from school with her head bowed. She had learned to walk with intention. With elegance.

On the evening of the party, a car arrived at her building promptly at seven. The driver opened the door without a word. Taylor stepped inside, her heart thudding with a rhythm both excited and uncertain.

The home was breathtaking. Lights twinkled from the branches of an ornamental tree that framed the entrance. Laughter floated through the hallways, accompanied by the clink of crystal and the muted thrum of chamber music.

Jaren greeted her at the door, his smile warm and disarming. "You look." He paused, genuinely struck. "Exquisite."

Taylor curtsied playfully. "I do hope I pass inspection."

He offered his arm. "You surpass it."

Together, they entered the grand room. Heads turned. Conversations paused briefly, curiosity flaring behind well-practiced expressions. Taylor kept her composure, chin high, spine straight. She smiled softly at those who met her gaze.

But then, she saw them.

Three figures moving with languid confidence, Jaren's friends. Kelly, with her practiced smirk and gleaming eyes. Kala, draped in couture, her tone of voice always one note from sarcasm. And Ervin, sharply dressed and forever calculating.

They approached.

"Well, well," Kelly drawled. "So, this is Taylor. Jaren has mentioned you."

Taylor extended her hand. "A pleasure."

Kala tilted her head. "That dress… is it vintage?"

"Possibly," Taylor replied with poise. "Good design has a way of transcending time."

Ervin leaned in slightly. "Tell us, Taylor, where did you attend university?"

Taylor's voice remained even. "A local college, close to home."

Kelly's smile widened. "Ah. Practical."

Taylor turned to Jaren, expecting him to step in, to deflect, to protect. But he laughed lightly and casually, as though the dagger were harmless.

The moment struck like a chord in a minor key. Her smile did not waver, but something inside her shifted. This was not unfamiliar. These were the hallways of her youth, repackaged in designer gowns and socialite manners.

She did not respond to their next remarks. Instead, she excused herself and stepped into a side room, a small library adorned with oil paintings and mahogany shelves. She stood there quietly, letting the hush of the room settle her nerves.

She thought of her father, of his belief in her worth, spoken not with grand gestures but with quiet, unwavering support. She closed her eyes and remembered his words.

"You do not need to convince anyone of your value. Your existence is the proof."

Outside the library, the laughter continued. But inside, Taylor stood in stillness, gathering strength from a well that had never run dry.

She returned to the party, eyes clear and spine unyielding. She would not bend to disdain. She had stitched herself together from too many torn pieces to unravel now.

As she walked past Kelly and the others, she offered a serene smile. "Thank you for your questions. They've reminded me that grace is never loud."

She returned to Jaren's side. He looked at her curiously, sensing a shift.

"Everything alright?"

Taylor nodded. "Yes. Quite."

But she knew now. She was not a guest in this world.

She was a revelation waiting to be reckoned with.

And she had just begun to unfold.

---

## Chapter 7: Silhouettes in the Foam

Taylor sat at her usual table by the café window, fingers curled gently around a porcelain cup. Outside, the city carried on in its usual, elegant motion. Inside, her cappuccino cooled slowly, its delicate foam art beginning to dissolve. She watched the silhouette fade, an angel this time perhaps, or a dancer mid-turn, until only a suggestion of its former shape remained.

It had been three days since the party. Three days of silence. Jaren had not called, nor texted. Taylor had not reached out either. She told herself she needed the quiet, but the absence pressed against her like an unwelcome shadow.

She sipped slowly, recalling each moment of that evening. The first glance, the shallow laughter, the barbed questions. And Jaren, standing just beside her, laughing with them. It had not been overt malice. But the quietness of his indifference had unsettled her more than she had expected. In that still room, the realization had struck her with perfect clarity. Jaren had not defended her because he did not think it necessary.

He had not understood the stakes. He had not seen the battlefield because for him, there was no war.

She opened her journal and began to write:

"They tried to reduce me with questions shaped like compliments. They asked me to define myself in terms they already understood. And when I did not comply, they diminished the shape of my silence. But I am not an echo to be interpreted. I am not their mirror."

She paused, her pen lingering above the page. A couple nearby laughed lightly over their croissants. The café's familiarity enveloped her, warm and calm. Yet within, she felt the unmistakable pull of unrest.

Her phone buzzed softly. A message.

**Jaren:** *Lunch today? My place? Miss your voice.*

Taylor stared at the screen. No mention of the party. No apology. No acknowledgment.

She set the phone aside. Then picked it up again.

**Taylor:** *I'll come. Noon.*

If he had nothing to say, then perhaps it was time he listened.

She arrived at the Best family's Manhattan penthouse promptly, as always. The doorman nodded, and the elevator whisked her to the upper floors. Everything was as she remembered. Tasteful, pristine, polished.

Jaren opened the door with a boyish grin. "You're early."

"I'm on time," she replied softly.

He leaned forward to kiss her cheek. She turned so that he met the edge of her jaw.

Undeterred, he gestured toward the dining alcove. "I had the chef prepare your favorite. Shall we?"

The table was perfectly set, down to the placement of a single orchid in a silver vase. But Taylor did not sit.

"I'd like to speak before we eat."

Jaren paused, then nodded slowly. "Of course."

Taylor clasped her hands in front of her. "Do you remember what Kelly asked me?"

He furrowed his brow, as if searching through irrelevant files. "She asked where you went to school. Something about your dress, too, I think."

"She mocked my background. My choices. Kala and Ervin joined in."

Jaren raised his hands slightly. "They were teasing. That's how they are. No harm meant."

Taylor inhaled slowly. "But harm was done."

"Taylor, you're strong. I didn't think you'd let that get to you."

"That is precisely the problem." Her voice was steady, low, and firm. "You see me as resilient enough to absorb anything. So, you allow it to happen."

He looked at her, not angry but confused. "I thought you understood my world. It's not always kind, but it's… it's ours."

"It's not mine," she said quietly. "Not if I have to diminish myself to remain within it."

He stepped closer. "I like you just as you are."

"But you do not protect me as I am."

Silence stretched between them.

"I came here today because I needed to hear what you would say when confronted. I needed to know whether you saw it."

"I didn't," he admitted. "I didn't know you felt so"

"Erased?" she offered.

He nodded slowly. "Yes."

Taylor reached into her satchel and withdrew her journal. She placed it on the table, closed.

"This is where I have lived most honestly. In pages you have never read."

He glanced at the journal but did not touch it.

"I wanted you to be a chapter in it," she continued. "Not a footnote."

"I still can be," he said. "We can work through this."

"Perhaps," she said. "But it must begin with understanding. And that requires more than charm."

Jaren nodded again, subdued. "You're not like anyone I've ever met."

"That is not a compliment," Taylor said gently. "It is a mirror."

She stepped back, lifting her chin with grace. "Thank you for lunch. Perhaps next time, we can begin again."

She turned and walked to the door. Behind her, the silence was more sincere than anything he had said aloud.

Back in the café later that afternoon, Taylor ordered her cappuccino with the same flair as always. But this time, when she received it, the foam art was different. A phoenix, wings outstretched, mid-ascent.

And she smiled.

Not because it was beautiful.

But because it was becoming.

**Chapter 8: Gold Dust and Razor Words**

Taylor stood before the boutique mirror once again, this time not in search of affirmation, but armor. Her fingers brushed over a deep navy gown adorned with gold-threaded embroidery. It was understated in color, but commanding in silhouette. The kind of dress that spoke before she did.

She had received another invitation from Jaren, an annual charity gala hosted by one of his oldest family friends. This time, Taylor accepted not for his sake, but for her own. She needed to return to that world, to look it in the eye and remind herself of her power within it.

The boutique attendant returned with a pair of matching heels, but Taylor was already dressed, smoothing the final line of fabric into place.

"You wear it as if it were tailored just for you," the woman said admiringly.

Taylor turned from the mirror, voice calm. "Thank you, I believe it was."

At the gala, a string quartet played somewhere just beyond the arched doorway, and laughter echoed through the ballroom, poised and rehearsed. Servers weaved through the crowd with silver trays, while glances flew across the room like currency.

Jaren met her at the entrance. "Taylor. You are luminous."

She smiled graciously. "Thank you. Shall we?"

They entered together, arm in arm, but Taylor's gaze was steady and unflinching. This was not enchantment. This was clarity.

It did not take long before the familiar trio approached. Kelly, all cheekbones and amusement, eyed Taylor with polite condescension. Kala, dressed in winter-white satin, offered a too-sweet smile. Ervin, with a glass of champagne already in hand, lingered with the predatory interest of someone expecting entertainment.

"Well," Kelly began, "isn't this a vision? I must say, Taylor, you've found your light."

Taylor inclined her head. "The light was always there. Some rooms simply reflect it better."

Kala laughed softly. "A poet, too. Tell me, how is junior college treating you these days?"

Taylor sipped her wine. "It treated me well enough to know that intelligence isn't measured in square footage or surnames."

Jaren cleared his throat lightly, a nervous reflex. Taylor felt the shift but did not flinch.

Ervin leaned in. "I think Taylor underestimates how refreshing her perspective is. It's not every day we're reminded how... grounded the world can be."

"Grounded," Taylor repeated. "Such an elegant substitute for condescension."

She set her glass down and met their eyes, one by one. Her voice remained serene, but her words sharpened like the edges of crystal.

"Let me save us all the effort. Yes, I went to a junior college. Yes, I grew up in a modest home, where books were borrowed, and shoes were polished by hand. And no, I do not share your pedigree. But I do share your presence, your posture, your privilege of being here. And I've done it without your validation."

The trio blinked, momentarily silenced.

Taylor smiled gently. "So, if we are to continue speaking, let us move past the illusions of superiority. Because silk threads do not weave character, and your laughter does not echo louder than my dignity."

Jaren looked as though he wished to interrupt, but Taylor gently touched his arm.

"Not tonight," she said. "This moment is mine."

She turned and walked toward the terrace, leaving behind the stunned expressions and the remnants of their carefully curated armor.

Outside, the evening air cooled her skin. The stars above blinked through the city haze. Taylor leaned against the marble railing and breathed deeply, her spine tall, her shoulders light.

A moment later, she sensed Jaren beside her.

"I didn't know what to say," he admitted.

"You did not have to say anything. You only had to stand beside me."

"I'm trying."

"I know," she replied. "But your world moves differently. It tests without reason, wounds without touch. I've learned to navigate it, but I cannot lose myself to stay within it."

He looked down, quiet. "You are extraordinary, Taylor."

"I am ordinary," she replied. "And that is where my strength lies."

Jaren turned toward her. "Then let me walk beside you in that strength."

Taylor studied him, her expression unreadable. "Only if you can do so without trying to define it."

They stood in silence, not as lovers swept in romance, but as two people standing on the edge of a truth they had only begun to understand.

Later, as Taylor returned home, she removed the gown with deliberate care. She placed it on its hanger, then stood before her mirror, examining not the dress, but the woman reflected within.

She was not the girl who once dreamed of being chosen.

She was the woman who had chosen herself.

And that truth sparkled brighter than diamonds ever could.

---

## Chapter 9: The Echo of Her Name

The sky wept softly as Taylor made her way down the familiar avenue toward the childhood home she had left behind. Her heels clicked lightly against the pavement, a subtle reminder that the woman she had become now walked through spaces the girl she once was could never have imagined. The autumn air carried the scent of rain-dampened leaves and something more distant, perhaps memory.

She had not returned to the neighborhood in years. Not since the funeral. Not since the echoes of her father's voice had been drowned by condolences and silence. But the time had come. Her mother had called that morning with a tremor in her voice, asking if she might come home, even just for a few hours. There was something she needed to give her. Something her father had left behind.

Taylor could not say no.

As she approached the modest two-story house with the white porch railing, she felt time slow. The windows were the same. The creak in the gate had not changed. And inside, the scent of lemon oil hung in the air like an inheritance.

Her mother met her at the door, arms opening before a word was spoken. The embrace was warm and familiar, and Taylor leaned into it with the reverence of someone returning to a sacred place.

"Come in, baby," her mother said, brushing a strand of hair from Taylor's face. "You must be tired."

"I'm alright, Mother. I just... needed to see this place again."

They sat in the living room, where the wallpaper had faded just slightly at the corners, and the floor creaked under their shifting weight. A fire burned softly in the hearth. Taylor's eyes moved across the room, absorbing each detail: the portrait of her father on the mantel, the cushion still indented where he used to sit, the bookshelf that tilted ever so slightly to the left.

"I found something," her mother said after a long silence. "It was tucked in the back of your father's desk. I think he meant to give it to you one day. But he never got the chance."

She rose and returned with a weathered envelope tied with a burgundy ribbon. Taylor accepted it with trembling hands. The paper was soft with age, but the ink on the front still read clearly: *To my daughter, when she is ready.*

Her mother quietly excused herself, giving her space.

Taylor opened the envelope with care, as if the message inside might dissolve in her hands. The letter was written in her father's meticulous script.

*"My dearest Taybird,

*If you are reading this, it means time has done what it always does, it moved forward. And I am not there to see the woman you've become. But I trust that she is remarkable.*

*I have watched you, from the moment you took your first breath to the day you read your first book and couldn't put it down. You were always curious, always kind. And though the world may not always return kindness in kind, I want you to know this: your gentleness is not a weakness. It is a quiet form of strength that most people will never understand.*

*I saw the way the world tried to overlook you, the way your light sometimes frightened people who lived in shadows. And I saw how you carried on anyway, quietly, gracefully. That is courage.*

*I know there will come a time when your heart will break. Perhaps it already has. But I need you to remember: a broken heart is still capable of love. Sometimes more so. It expands through the cracks, not in spite of them, but because of them.*

*If you ever feel small, or unworthy, or uncertain, read this and remember who you are. You are the daughter of a man who believed, without doubt or hesitation, that you were destined for something beautiful.*

*Stand tall, Taybird. Speak clearly. Love fiercely. And when in doubt, remember that I am with you, in every quiet moment, in every rising sun, and in every echo of your name.*

Love, Dad"

By the end, Taylor's hands shook. Tears slipped down her cheeks in silent procession. Her breath came shallow, as though the very air could not hold the weight of her grief.

She pressed the letter to her chest and closed her eyes. The living room around her blurred. In her mind, she saw his face again, not as it was in the hospital bed, but as it had been on the mornings he made her tea, in the way he whistled while reading the paper, in the softness of his voice when he told her she mattered.

The sob escaped before she could stop it. It was not a cry of despair, but of longing. Of love that had nowhere left to go.

Her mother returned without a word, settled beside her, and wrapped her arms around her child. They rocked gently, mother and daughter, a single breath between them.

"Thank you," Taylor whispered, her voice raw.

"I miss him every day," her mother replied, voice trembling.

"So, do I. So do I."

That night, Taylor stayed in her childhood room. The walls, once filled with posters and bookmarks, now held only memories. She placed the letter beside her pillow and stared at the ceiling, where shadows danced with the flicker of the fireplace.

She remembered being ten, hiding in the closet after school, muffling tears with the sleeve of her cardigan. She remembered her father finding her, kneeling beside her, and simply staying there, saying nothing, holding her until the sobs stopped. He had not told her to be strong. He had shown her how.

Taylor rose and walked to the window. Outside, the rain had stopped. The streetlights glistened against the wet pavement. She opened the window and let the cool air in.

Somewhere in the quiet, she whispered, "I'm trying, Dad. I'm really trying."

The wind stirred, gentle and affirming.

And in the stillness, she felt it: the echo of her name.

Not shouted. Not claimed. Simply spoken with love.

She turned back to her bed, lay down, and closed her eyes.

Sleep came slowly, but when it did, it carried no nightmares. Only light. Only memory. Only peace.

And in the morning, when Taylor rose, she did not just carry herself forward. She carried the legacy of a man who believed she could change the world.

And for the first time in a long time, she believed it too.

---

## Chapter 10: Dissonance in D Minor

The city was quiet that morning, as though holding its breath. Taylor stood by the tall windows of her apartment, watching the rain trace slow rivers down the glass. Outside, umbrellas bloomed like dark flowers, and the world moved forward in muted tones. But inside, something within her had stilled. Not from peace, but from pressure. The kind of quiet that builds before a note is struck.

A package had arrived earlier that morning, wrapped in cream paper with a thin navy ribbon. No note. No sender. She had known, instantly, that it was from Jaren.

Inside was a first-edition copy of her favorite novel, bound in deep burgundy leather and embossed in gold. Tucked within its pages was a single sheet of stationery, bearing just a few lines in Jaren's precise script.

"Sometimes words fail us. Let this speak what I cannot."

Taylor closed the book carefully and set it aside. She had not seen Jaren since the gala. Not since she had peeled back the veil of his world with words as deliberate as they were necessary. The memory of that night clung to her, not with anger, but with sadness. There had been a silence in him she had hoped to fill. A silence that, now, she realized was his to address.

She sat at her piano, untouched for months, and let her fingers hover over the keys. Her father had taught her to play. Music had been their shared language when words had felt insufficient. He used to say that every person had a signature key, the one in which their soul sang.

Hers had always been D minor.

She began to play.

The melody was hesitant at first, fingers trembling, but it gathered shape quickly. It was not a song she had learned. It was one she remembered from a dream, or perhaps a moment when the heart composed on its own.

Each note was a memory: the scent of her father's jacket, the warmth of his hand on her shoulder, the way her mother smiled in the doorway when Taylor played.

She played until the tears blurred her vision, and even then, she did not stop.

That afternoon, her mother called. The voice on the other end was gentler than usual, and Taylor sensed immediately that something was wrong.

"Is everything alright, Mom?"

A pause. Then, "Your aunt called from overseas. She's not well. And I can't get a flight to her in time."

Taylor listened quietly.

"She was asking for your father. She doesn't know, baby. She's lost track of the years. I tried to explain, but it's like she's walking backward through her mind."

Taylor's throat tightened. "I'll go."

"Are you sure? It's a long journey. And she may not recognize you."

"Then I'll remind her."

The flight to Marseille France was long and shrouded in gray skies. Taylor sat near the window, her journal in her lap. She wrote in slow, deliberate strokes, capturing thoughts that refused to be spoken aloud. Her seatmate said nothing, sensing her solitude was not loneliness but necessity.

By the time she arrived at the coastal hospice where her aunt stayed, twilight had begun to settle. The building was a pale stone villa, its windows glowing with soft lamplight. A nurse met her at the entrance, kind-eyed and steady.

"She has moments of clarity," the nurse said gently. "And moments of retreat. Don't be discouraged."

Taylor nodded, stepping into the hallway.

Her aunt's room was quiet. The woman who once traveled the world with a camera around her neck and a satchel full of maps now sat in a chair by the window, her frame delicate beneath a woolen shawl.

"Aunt May," Taylor said softly.

The woman turned. Her eyes, though clouded, fixed on Taylor's face.

"You're late," she said, smiling faintly.

Taylor blinked. "You remember me?"

"Of course. You're the only one who listens without waiting to speak."

Taylor approached slowly, kneeling beside her. "I came as soon as I could."

They spoke for hours, their conversation a thread of memories and half-truths, woven together with affection. May recalled stories that never happened, and Taylor listened as if they had. Occasionally, her aunt would remember, briefly and brilliantly, the people they had loved and lost.

"He was so proud of you," May said once, her fingers tightening around Taylor's. "Your father. He wrote me letters every month. Said you were his greatest masterpiece."

Taylor could not answer. The words caught in her throat.

"I'm tired," her aunt whispered. "But you're here. That's enough."

Taylor stayed through the night. When May slept, she sat beside her, writing by candlelight. She wrote about the silence between piano notes. About the dignity of aging. About the grace of a woman who had once seen the world and now waited for the world to return to her.

In the morning, May passed away. Peacefully. With Taylor holding her hand.

The days that followed were blurred with arrangements and farewells. Taylor wandered through Marseille's narrow streets, listening to the sea, watching how the wind carried voices from one shore to the next. She visited an old cathedral, lit a candle, and sat in stillness.

She thought of Jaren. Of the piano. Of her father's letter.

Of all the ways love whispered itself into permanence.

On the flight home, Taylor looked out over the Atlantic. The clouds below looked like pages yet to be written. Her journal lay open on the tray table.

"There are songs we carry that no one else hears. But that does not make them any less real. My dissonance is not a flaw. It is my harmony."

When she arrived home, the city greeted her with familiar indifference. But Taylor moved through it differently now. Not louder. Just fuller. She returned to the café, sat at her usual table, and ordered her cappuccino.

The barista greeted her with a nod. "Foam art request today?"

Taylor thought for a moment. "Surprise me."

She sipped her drink slowly. The foam depicted a violin bow arcing across strings. She smiled.

At home, she returned to the piano. She placed her hands gently on the keys and played the melody she had begun days before. This time, it did not tremble.

It rose.

In D minor.

And it carried every goodbye, every letter, every echo of her name.

Taylor closed her eyes and played until the room filled with the music of all she had lost, and all she had found.

And when she finally stopped, she wept.

Not for sorrow.

But for having held the note long enough to let it go.

---

## Chapter 11: Lamb Among Lions

The morning air was damp with the scent of something unsettled. Even the sun seemed reluctant to rise, hiding behind a thick veil of clouds that cast the world in an expectant hush. Taylor stood at the curb outside the Best family estate, her coat drawn tightly around her, as if bracing not just for the chill but for what she might face inside. A black town car idled nearby. The driver, gloved and wordless, opened the door for her with practiced precision.

This was not a gala. Not a banquet. Jaren had extended a different invitation this time. A private brunch, one reserved for inner-circle confidants, family loyalists, and the kind of political allies who did not exchange business cards but legacies. It was the Best family's annual Who's Who gathering, where invitations were less about inclusion and more about hierarchy.

Taylor had hesitated. Her heart told her to decline. Her instincts whispered that she did not belong. And yet, something stronger nudged her forward. Not curiosity. Not even loyalty. Something else. A sense that the answers she needed might be waiting beyond those towering estate doors.

The car slowed to a stop in front of the grand portico. Taylor inhaled deeply. She touched her gloves, forest green and soft against her skin, and remembered what her father once said. A lion does not roar to frighten. A lion roars to be known.

Inside, the estate was alive with quiet elegance. Staff moved like shadows, adjusting table settings and lighting candles in sconces. The house breathed wealth, but more than that, it pulsed with the tension of secrets. Every step Taylor took echoed through the marbled corridors like a whispered question.

The brunch was set in the solarium, a sun-drenched expanse of glass and ivory linen. Orchids lined the center of the long table. Crystal reflected the morning light like tiny stars. Taylor walked with poise, every movement measured. She greeted the guests, noting the subtle glances, the practiced smiles, the veiled interest.

She was seated near the center, beside Jaren. Across from them sat Kelly, her smile as polished as her pearls. Kala followed shortly behind, draped in an alabaster shawl that did little to soften her gaze. Ervin joined them with a champagne flute in hand, offering Taylor a nod that bordered on predatory.

Conversations began, urbane and measured. Taylor kept her posture tall and her responses brief. She allowed herself to observe. To listen. The quiet clink of cutlery, the hum of distant music, and the occasional rise of laughter created a soundscape of curated civility.

"So, Taylor," Kelly began sweetly as she adjusted her place card. "How have you been occupying your time lately? Still immersed in your... community projects?"

Taylor sipped her tea. "Yes. There is fulfillment in work that touches real lives."

"Of course," Kala added with a smile that did not reach her eyes. "Though I imagine such efforts come with their own... challenges."

"They do," Taylor replied. "But they also come with clarity."

Mr. Best sat at the head of the table, watching. His silence spoke louder than his words ever could. Mrs. Best, poised and unreadable, gave Taylor a nod that felt like approval.

When the main course was served, Taylor excused herself under the pretense of freshening up. She moved through the house with quiet purpose, hoping to escape the weight of scrutiny. Her heels led her down a hallway lined with portraits, toward a side room she had not entered before.

It was a library, dimly lit and rich with the scent of leather and mahogany. She stepped inside, closing the door gently behind her, craving a moment to breathe. But before she could exhale, voices reached her.

There was another door. Slightly ajar. Beyond it, an inner office.

She heard Mr. Best's voice first. Commanding. Impatient.

"This shipment cannot be delayed again. The cost is irrelevant. The consequences are not."

Another voice followed. Gravelly, foreign. Mr. Phillips.

"The mines are collapsing. We are losing over fifty people, including children, a day. If we continue to operate without the protection of legitimate contracts, the government will shut us down. Or worse."

Taylor froze. Her breath caught.

Blood diamonds.

She had heard the term before, in passing. But never imagined it would trace back to this house. To this family.

Then came Jaren's voice. Clear. Clipped. Unrecognizable.

"We do not care about the workers. They are not the asset. The shipment is."

The words landed like stone against glass. Taylor's knees weakened.

She stepped backward, her hand instinctively covering her mouth. A sound escaped her, small, but not unnoticed.

Inside, the conversation halted.

"What was that?" Mr. Phillips asked.

Taylor moved quickly. She darted toward the outer door of the library but hesitated when she spotted Kelly and Ervin just down the corridor, laughing at nothing, their eyes scanning the space.

She could not leave without being seen.

She pressed herself into a corner behind a velvet drape and waited. The adjoining door creaked. Taylor held her breath. Footsteps entered the library. Heavy. Deliberate.

"Nothing," Mr. Phillips muttered. "But be careful. These walls are not as silent as you think."

He exited.

Taylor waited several more moments before moving. Her body was trembling. Her mind raced.

She slipped back into the hallway, then down toward the nearest restroom. Inside, she leaned against the door, trying to steady herself. The mirror offered no comfort. Only reflection.

Who was this man she was falling for? Who were these people?

She left the restroom composed, her expression calm. She would not fall apart here.

As she moved toward the front of the house, she saw her opportunity. Guests had begun to shift toward the drawing room. The hallway cleared.

She made her way toward the exit.

Just before she reached the door, a familiar voice called out.

"Taylor?"

It was Mrs. Best.

Taylor turned.

"Are you leaving?" the woman said warmly.

Taylor managed a soft smile. "Yes. I wasn't feeling well. I hope it's alright."

"Of course," Mrs. Best said. Her eyes lingered. "You take care."

Taylor nodded and stepped outside.

The air hit her like absolution.

Her car pulled around. She climbed in, closed the door, and finally let herself exhale.

When she reached home, she opened her journal.

She began to write.

Every name. Every quote. Every horror.

When she finished, she stared at the final line she had written.

"They do not expect the lamb to rise. But they will remember the roar."

Taylor arrived at her apartment and pushed through the front door with trembling urgency. The moment the door clicked shut behind her, she collapsed to the floor, sliding down the wood with her back pressed hard against it. Her fingers clutched her purse and keys like lifelines, her breath leaving her body in a sharp gasp.

The silence of her home offered no comfort. It only amplified the chaos within her.

She tried to make sense of what she had heard, the voices, the words, the absence of remorse. She replayed Jaren's tone, searching for a crack, a hesitation, anything that would redeem him. But the memory was clear. His voice had been calm. Certain. Cold.

Still, her mind resisted.

Perhaps he had been caught in something larger. Perhaps he was protecting his family. Perhaps… perhaps.

And then came the memory.

One of many, but this one arrived with cruel clarity. Jaren's friends, circling her like wolves dressed in silk, their words sharpened with practiced cruelty. And Jaren, not silent in discomfort, but smiling. Not unaware, but entertained.

The flash was brief, but it struck with precision.

She began to peel back the layers of their relationship. Each moment examined not through the veil of hope, but in the bare light of truth.

They had been beautiful when alone. But never whole. Around others, Jaren changed. Around others, he seemed amused by her discomfort. Pleased, even, to watch her navigate their cruel games.

Her chest tightened.

She let out a second gasp, this one soaked in disbelief. A tear followed, carving a slow, deliberate path down her cheek.

She had allowed herself to believe in him. In who she thought he was. Not because he had shown her, but because she needed someone to be that for her. He had become a version she curated in her heart, sculpted from longing and soft-spoken moments that never truly stood up to the noise of the world.

More tears came. Not just of grief, but of clarity.

She wrapped her arms around her body, folding into herself as though her own embrace might hold her together. Her back against the door, her knees pulled close, she rocked gently, the rhythm of pain quiet but present.

The room dimmed around her. Time softened.

And somewhere between mourning and surrender, Taylor fell asleep on the floor, curled into the silence.

When morning came, it found her in that same place, the weight of truth resting across her shoulders like a new skin.

But something had shifted.

The girl who had collapsed against the door had vanished with the night.

The woman who opened her eyes was not broken.

She was becoming.

---

## Chapter 12: Keys to Secrets

The sky over the Hudson hung low, a slate-colored hush that mirrored the unease simmering just beneath Taylor's skin. It had been two weeks since the brunch at the Best estate. Since she had looked Mr. Best in the eye and spoken truth to a man used to sculpting his world with power. Since Jaren's mother had taken her hand and confirmed what Taylor had always suspected, that grace was stronger than grandeur.

Now, as Taylor stood once again at the edge of that estate's long stone driveway, she felt something new humming beneath her breath. It wasn't fear. It wasn't even resolve. It was something heavier. Something purposeful.

She had a plan.

The call she had made to Jaren the day before had been simple.

"Lunch on the terrace?" she'd asked.

"Of course," he'd replied, a smile audible in his voice. "I thought you might be done with us."

"Not done. Just beginning."

Now she was here. A deep navy coat clung to her shoulders, and beneath it, the journal that had held her thoughts, her dreams, her wounds, her scars, for more than a decade.

The driver escorted her through the great entryway. Taylor walked with slow precision, each step quiet but deliberate. She passed the grand staircase, the towering floral arrangements, the portraits of Best patriarchs whose eyes seemed to follow her. And then she arrived.

The terrace was bathed in autumn light. Jaren stood waiting, dressed more casually than usual, a light sweater over pressed trousers. He looked younger, less armored.

"You look radiant," he said as she approached.

Taylor smiled, but her eyes held a question.

"You're alone?"

He gestured to the table. "Just us. As promised."

They sat. For a few moments, they spoke softly of small things. The weather. Books. A recent art exhibit. Taylor watched him closely, noting the easy rhythm of his voice. He had always known how to make people feel comfortable. It was part of the charm. Part of the danger.

"I want to show you something," she said at last.

Jaren leaned forward slightly. "Alright."

Taylor opened her journal and turned to a page near the back. Inside it, she had written everything she remembered from the conversation she'd overheard weeks ago. The one in the inner office. The one about blood diamonds, about workers dying, about shipments and laundering.

She didn't hand him the journal. She simply read from it.

Jaren said nothing at first. But the color drained slightly from his face.

"You were there," he said finally.

"I was."

His voice dropped. "You weren't meant to hear that."

"No one was."

They sat in silence.

Then Jaren ran a hand through his hair, the way he did when his confidence frayed.

"That world… it wasn't supposed to touch you."

"But it did. And now I have to decide what to do with it."

His eyes darkened. "Taylor, this isn't a game. There are people, powerful people, who wouldn't hesitate to protect their interests."

"I know."

"Then why are you here?"

"Because I need to know who you are. The real you. Not the version I met at a café with gold-dusted cappuccino foam. The one who stood by as I was mocked. The one who said nothing while children mine stones for your family's wealth."

He flinched.

"I didn't want you to be part of that," he said. "That's why I never let you in completely."

Taylor nodded. "But you did. Because I walked in anyway."

He leaned forward, urgent now. "What do you want, Taylor? If it's money, if it's security"

"I want the truth."

She stood and walked toward the French doors that led back into the house. She paused.

"There's a key I need," she said without turning around. "To the inner office. The one behind your father's study. I believe it holds records. Ledgers. Proof."

Jaren's silence stretched thin.

"Why would I give you that?"

Taylor turned, her voice quiet but sharp. "Because if you ever loved me at all, even a fraction of what I felt for you, then you'll help me stop this."

He said nothing.

That evening, long after she had returned to her apartment, a small package arrived. Inside was a key, wrapped in linen, and a note.

"I'm not the man I thought I was. But maybe this is a start." J.

Taylor sat on her bed, the key in her palm. It felt heavier than it should have. Weighted by legacy, by pain, by choice.

The next morning, she returned.

She dressed plainly. No makeup. No artifice. Just Taylor.

She slipped through the halls quietly, the key hidden in her coat pocket. She passed staff without comment. No one stopped her.

At the door to the office, she paused. Her breath came in quiet waves. She inserted the key.

Click.

The door creaked open.

Inside, it smelled of leather and old ambition. Shelves lined with books that had never been read. Cabinets sealed with brushed brass. A mahogany desk that seemed to stretch the width of the room.

She searched.

Every drawer. Every folder. Until she found them.

Ledger books. Shipment documents. Transactions that funneled funds from African mining operations to shell corporations to charitable foundations bearing the Best name.

Names. Dates. Accounts.

Proof.

And then she heard it.

The soft click of heels behind her.

Taylor turned.

Mrs. Best stood in the doorway, her eyes calm.

"I thought you might come," she said.

"You knew?"

Mrs. Best stepped inside, closing the door behind her.

"I've known for years. But he never let me close enough. I needed someone who could."

They looked at each other.

"What do we do?" Taylor asked.

Mrs. Best walked to the desk and lifted a pen. She placed it gently in Taylor's hand.

"We write the ending ourselves."

Taylor nodded, her throat tight.

Tears slipped down her cheeks as she opened her journal and began to copy names, dates, balances.

And for the first time, her hand did not tremble.

Not because she wasn't afraid.

But because she had something greater than fear.

She had purpose.

And a key that opened more than just doors.

It opened the truth.

---

## Chapter 13: Stillness at the Door

There is a silence that comes before great change. Not the kind that comforts, but the kind that listens. That morning, Taylor sat at her desk long after the sun had risen, bathed in amber light, unmoving. The journal lay closed. The key had done its part. The secrets were no longer just suspicions but evidence. And with that knowledge came a burden heavier than any she had carried.

Her phone remained unanswered. Jaren had called four times the night before. He had not left a message. But she knew what he wanted. Perhaps an explanation. Perhaps absolution. Perhaps to erase what had been written in the ledgers she now held like a map to an empire built on silence and sacrifice.

But there was no more room for erasure. Not in her world.

The plan had taken shape in the hours before dawn. It was not born of vengeance. Taylor did not believe in revenge. She believed in reckoning.

Her first stop was a law office just off Madison Avenue. She had made the appointment anonymously. A woman with influence and intention. She arrived early. The receptionist barely looked up before leading her to a conference room where a junior partner awaited.

She placed the envelope on the table.

"I need this protected," she said. "If anything happens to me, I need you to make it public."

The man opened the envelope, and as he read the first page, his face paled.

"Is this real?"

Taylor met his gaze. "Every line."

"Do you know what you're holding?"

"Yes. Do you?"

He nodded slowly. "These could bring down a corporation. An entire family dynasty."

"Then they should."

From there, Taylor walked. Past bookstores. Past bakeries where the scent of fresh bread mixed with exhaust. Past a florist trimming the ends of white roses. She did not rush. She wanted to feel the city one last time before she changed it.

Her next meeting was with an investigative journalist. A woman who had once won awards but now published independently, having grown tired of editorial red tape. They met in a quiet tea house where the clinking of porcelain disguised the gravity of their exchange.

"I've been waiting for something like this," the journalist said. "Do you want to be named?"

"No," Taylor replied. "Not yet."

"Then what do you want?"

"Truth," she said. "In print. In air. On screens. Everywhere."

The woman smiled. "I can do that."

Taylor returned home as dusk began to gather the city into its arms. Her apartment was quiet. Safe. But no longer small. It had become a sanctuary where courage had grown, quietly, word by word.

She changed into a simple gray dress and wrapped a shawl around her shoulders. She sat at the piano again. Her fingers hovered above the keys.

Then came the knock.

She knew it would be him. There was no urgency in it. Only stillness.

She opened the door.

Jaren stood there, coat unbuttoned, his expression unreadable.

"Can I come in?"

Taylor stepped aside. He walked in slowly, stopping at the edge of the living room.

"I know what you've done," he said.

"I know," she replied.

He turned to face her fully. "Do you hate me?"

She shook her head. "No. I pity the man who chose silence when he could have chosen something more."

"I didn't know how to fix it."

"You still don't. But I do."

He sat on the edge of the couch, his hands clasped.

"I never meant to hurt you."

"But you did. Not by acting, but by standing still."

They sat in the quiet.

Finally, he said, "They'll come for you. If the story goes live, they won't care who you are."

Taylor stood straighter. "Let them come. I've lived through worse than shadows."

Jaren rose. "You could run. I could help you disappear."

"But I'm not disappearing. I'm arriving."

He nodded. "Then let me help. I can testify. I can give names."

"You can," she said. "But you have to decide whether you're doing it for justice or for redemption."

He looked at her, his eyes red-rimmed. "Maybe both."

She did not offer him forgiveness. That was not hers to give. But she offered him the door.

"Then start with this."

She handed him a page torn from her journal. It was a list of contacts. People hurt. People silenced. People erased.

"Speak for them. Then we'll talk about speaking for you."

He took the page. Folded it. Pocketed it.

"I never knew what strength looked like until I met you," he said.

Taylor's voice was calm. "Strength is not noise. It's truth. Even when it trembles."

When he left, the stillness returned. But it was no longer heavy.

It was holy.

Taylor turned to the piano and played.

Not for memory. Not for mourning.

She played because there was still music in her.

And the door had been opened.

Not to escape.

But to walk through.

Ready.

## Chapter 14: Lessons from a Narcissist

It was nearly midnight when Taylor returned to her journal. The apartment was quiet, save for the steady tick of the wall clock and the occasional moan of wind brushing the windows. She sat at her desk, hands folded neatly atop blank pages. The key to the Best estate office now rested inside a drawer, locked away like the secrets it had revealed. And yet, Taylor could not sleep. Her mind, once a sanctuary, now teetered between resolve and raw disbelief.

Jaren had left just hours ago, carrying with him the names of those buried beneath the Best fortune. Whether he would truly speak for them, Taylor did not know. And she would not wait to find out.

She opened her journal and wrote with a steadiness she did not yet feel:

*"To betray oneself is the deepest cruelty. And to watch someone you once loved to do it with charm is the education no one wants but everyone remembers."*

She stopped, exhaled slowly, and turned the page.

When she was a child, Taylor believed people told the truth by accident. That in time, masks fell not from force, but from fatigue. What she had not accounted for were those who wore their deceit as identity. Not hidden. Not ashamed. But practiced and refined like a signature.

She thought of Jaren.

The charming introductions. The grand gestures. The way he had studied her in the beginning, not with curiosity, but with calculation. How he mirrored her dreams, echoed her values, until she began to believe they shared a rhythm. She now knew it was a performance. Polished. Strategic.

What stunned her most was not that he had deceived others, but that he had deceived himself.

She heard a knock at the door.

Not urgent. Deliberate.

Taylor froze.

No one visited her this late. She rose quietly, her pulse loud in her ears, and crossed the room. She did not open the door immediately. Instead, she asked:

"Who is it?"

A woman's voice answered. Steady. Clear.

"My name is Isabel Marchand. I believe we have a shared interest. And perhaps a shared enemy."

Taylor opened the door.

Standing in the hallway was a woman dressed in tailored black, her eyes sharp, her presence unmistakable. She carried a leather portfolio in one hand, her other rested lightly at her side.

"May I come in?"

Taylor stepped aside. Isabel entered without hesitation. She moved like someone used to rooms bending around her.

"I've read the story," she said, sitting before being asked. "Or at least, the parts your journalist has chosen to preview. It's good. You've done well."

Taylor closed the door. "And you are?"

Isabel opened her portfolio. Inside were photos. Documents. Pages stamped with foreign insignias.

"I used to work for a regulatory agency in Geneva. Until I was offered a very large sum to stop asking questions."

Taylor narrowed her gaze. "About the Best family?"

"About their holdings. About the mines. About the funds passing through shell companies like wine through crystal."

Taylor sat slowly across from her. "Why now?"

"Because your story is about to open a door that will expose more than you realize. And I suspect you do not yet know how far the corridor goes."

Taylor's voice was quiet. "Enlighten me."

Isabel spread out a page across the table. It was a map. A diagram of corporate ownerships, names tied to faces, charities tied to offshore accounts.

"There is more than diamonds," Isabel said. "Much more. There are technologies. Arms deals. Political bribes. And all of it is under the same name."

Taylor felt the room tilt slightly. "And you've come to me because?"

"Because I want this exposed. I have tried. Alone, I was silenced. But you are already speaking."

"Exactly."

The two women sat in mutual silence, the weight of knowing pressing down on them.

"Jaren," Taylor said after a pause. "Was he involved?"

Isabel looked up. "Not directly. But he knew. And when asked to stay silent, he did."

Taylor swallowed. "And what about now?"

Isabel's face softened. "That remains to be seen."

The clock ticked louder than before.

Taylor stood. "Then we go together. We tell everything."

Isabel nodded. "But carefully. They are watching now."

The following day unfolded like a chessboard. Taylor met with the journalist, handed over the expanded files, watched as the woman's eyes widened at the sheer scope of what lay before her.

"We'll serialize it," she said. "They won't know what to fight first."

Back at her apartment, Taylor received a message.

It was from Jaren.

"You have more allies than you realize. Some are closer than you think. Be careful. I'm sorry."

She didn't respond.

That evening, Taylor took the train to visit a woman named Nora Jensen, the widow of a man whose name had appeared in one of the ledgers. Nora lived in a quiet suburb, in a home filled with books and fading photographs. She answered the door with tired eyes and welcomed Taylor without hesitation.

"I knew someone would come eventually," she said, pouring tea into china cups.

Taylor explained her purpose. Showed the documents. Nora read without blinking.

"My husband tried to speak," she said. "He was threatened. Then he disappeared. They ruled it a car accident. I never believed it."

Taylor reached across the table. "We're going to tell your story."

Tears welled in Nora's eyes. "Do it for him. For all of them."

On the train ride home, Taylor wrote in her journal.

*"A narcissist does not fear being hated. Only being exposed. And now, the light is coming."*

But even as she returned to her apartment, she sensed it. A change in the air. A threat not named, but nearby.

Her front door had been opened. Not broken. Not forced. Just unlocked.

She stepped inside cautiously. Nothing was stolen. But something was missing.

The key.

Gone.

Taylor sank into the nearest chair, her body trembling.

They had found her.

She wasn't safe.

But she wasn't finished either.

That night, she stayed awake until the city itself fell silent. She contacted Isabel, arranged a secure place to meet. She contacted the journalist, told her to hold the next release until they were certain.

And then, as the moon climbed high, Taylor began to write again.

"I am not the girl in the hallway anymore. I am the voice at the end of the corridor. I am the reckoning."

The truth had a price.

She was ready to pay it.

---

## Chapter 15: Operation Payback

The wind howled across the Hudson, rattling the windows of Taylor's apartment as though the sky itself demanded entry. She stood in the kitchen, pouring a cup of tea, her hands steady despite the electric tension twisting in her chest. Operation Payback was no longer just an idea. It was in motion.

Across the city, secrets were shifting. The journalist was readying the first full publication. Files had been delivered to legal offices, whistleblower organizations, and media contacts who now buzzed with the promise of exposure. But Taylor knew that a spotlight that bright could also cast shadows deep enough to swallow a person whole.

She looked up as a knock echoed from the door. This time, she had been expecting it.

Mrs. Best stepped inside with grace. She wore a long gray coat and held her clutch like a ledger. Her presence always carried dignity, but tonight there was something different. Her eyes were alert, her voice lower than usual.

"I had to see you in person," she said, stepping into the warmth. "It's time."

Taylor nodded. "Yes. I'm ready."

They sat by the fire, and for a long moment, neither woman spoke. The room glowed with amber light, flickering against the spine of Taylor's journal that rested on the coffee table.

"I've spoken to the board," Mrs. Best began, her voice calm. "I have the votes to force a transition. Quietly, if possible. But this story you've sparked, it's not going to remain quiet."

"It shouldn't," Taylor said. "They deserve the noise. Every name. Every lie."

Mrs. Best sipped her tea. "Do you know what he said to me, the night Jaren was born? Mr. Best said, 'We will raise a dynasty. One that cannot fall.'"

Taylor's lips tightened. "And yet it is crumbling."

Mrs. Best looked into the flames. "I didn't know the details until years later. I suspected, but he kept his business so layered, so carefully orchestrated, even I could not unwind it. Not without consequence."

"You were protecting yourself?"

"I was protecting Jaren. Or so I told myself. But denial is a form of betrayal, as well."

The silence between them settled heavily. Then Taylor leaned forward.

"What made you change?"

Mrs. Best looked at her with a gaze full of ghosts. "You. You reminded me of who I used to be. Before I became the woman who attended galas and looked away. You reminded me that silence is not safety."

Taylor's voice was soft. "Then we change it together."

They spoke for another hour. They charted out the transition. The board's vote. The statements. The succession that would remove Mr. Best and prevent Jaren from inheriting the criminal structure beneath the Best empire. And as they talked, Taylor's resolve deepened.

As Mrs. Best stood to leave, she placed a hand gently on Taylor's shoulder.

"You know," she said, "you've done what no one else could. Not just uncover truth, but transform it."

Taylor looked up. "How do you mean?"

Mrs. Best smiled, a sorrowful curl of her lips. "You've shown them what happens when the quiet woman speaks. When the girl they ignored becomes the architect of their downfall."

Taylor exhaled.

Mrs. Best continued. "It's fitting, don't you think? That title you're keeping for the journalist's series. I believe you called it **The Harder They Fall.**"

Taylor blinked, tears welling. "It was never about revenge. It was about showing the world who really stands tall."

Mrs. Best nodded. "And the irony, my dear, is that you rose by making others accountable. You didn't roar. You endured."

After she left, Taylor stood at the window, watching the night wrap itself around the city. She whispered the words to herself.

**The Harder They Fall.**

The next morning, news broke.

Screens lit up across the country with headlines linking the Best empire to human rights violations, illegal trade, money laundering. Jaren's face was not the one in the headlines, but his name was there. A quiet mention. Enough to stain.

Taylor had not returned his messages.

But she saw him later that day.

He came to the café. The same one where they had once stood side by side, ordering cappuccinos like declarations of belonging. Today, he stood behind her in silence.

She turned.

"I read it," he said. "All of it."

"I know."

He looked pale. Worn.

"I didn't think you'd go through with it."

"I never stopped thinking about the ones who had no voice."

He nodded. "It's not over, you know. My father will fight this."

"I expect him to. But I'm not afraid of men who only know how to threaten."

"I wanted to be different," Jaren said, his voice cracking. "I really did. I just didn't know how, maybe I was too afraid under my father's shadow."

Taylor's eyes were gentle. "Then become someone else. No one's stopping you."

Jaren responded, "But how?" He looked down, then left without another word.

The next few weeks passed in a whirlwind.

Taylor testified anonymously in front of legal panels. Her files became casework. Her interviews were reviewed by watchdog groups and international law experts. People began to speak. Former employees. Journalists. Survivors.

The storm had come.

And through it all, Taylor stood calm. Resolute.

One evening, she received a letter. Handwritten. From the sister of a miner who had died in one of the documented operations. The letter simply said:

"You gave him back to me. Thank you."

Taylor read it three times. She placed it inside her journal.

Her voice had made someone feel seen. And that, she knew, was power.

Not control. Not dominance.

Humanity.

That same night, Taylor sat once again at her piano. The fire beside her crackled low. Her fingers touched the keys, and for the first time in many months, she played not from pain, but from peace.

A simple song. Just notes.

But each one sang with clarity.

Her door, once closed in fear, now stood open.

And from beyond it, the world waited.

Not to save her.

But to hear her.

She had become the reckoning.

And the melody of that truth would never again be silenced.

## Chapter 16: The Boutique of Becoming

The morning light slipped through the cracks in the curtains like quiet promises. Taylor rose from her bed with a sense of stillness she hadn't felt in months. Her body moved slowly, as if recognizing the change before her mind could name it. She washed her face, brushed her hair, and made a cup of jasmine tea, the steam curling upward like incense for a life that was finally beginning to breathe again.

There had been battles behind her. Conversations etched in memory. Files delivered, stories told, lives honored. But today, Taylor did something she hadn't allowed herself since the beginning.

She opened her closet.

It had always been orderly. Hangers spaced with discipline, colors moving from dark to light. But today, she did not search for neutrality. She was not hiding. She reached instead for a dress she had once believed belonged to another version of herself. One she would never be allowed to become.

It was soft ivory, with delicate lace sleeves and a neckline that curved like a whispered blessing. She held it in her hands for a long moment.

This was the dress she had tried on all those months ago in the boutique where she had first decided to walk boldly into Jaren's world. She had purchased it with trembling fingers and worn it with trembling resolve.

That night, she had been mocked, belittled, and betrayed.

But she hadn't returned the dress.

Today, she wore it again. Not for them. Not for him.

For her.

Outside, the city pulsed beneath a sky brushed with blue. Taylor stepped into the boutique she had once entered in quiet desperation. The chime above the door rang sweetly.

A different woman stood behind the counter now, younger, though no less elegant. She greeted Taylor with a warm smile.

"Welcome back."

Taylor looked around. The displays shimmered with silks and satins, but what caught her eye was a small dressing mirror in the corner. She walked toward it, remembering how she had once turned from her reflection. Today, she faced it.

Her image met her eyes without apology.

"Do you need help with anything?" the attendant asked.

"No," Taylor replied. "I just came to see her."

She placed a hand lightly on the mirror. Then, after a pause, she added, "She's come a long way."

The woman tilted her head but said nothing. Taylor smiled and left the boutique without looking back.

Her next stop was the school.

It had taken courage to reach out. The principal at her old junior college had responded quickly to her email, expressing not only gratitude for her recent advocacy work, but genuine interest in her returning. Not as a student.

As a guest speaker.

Now she stood outside the very building where she had spent long afternoons in quiet corners, never quite seen. Today, she was ushered into an auditorium filled with students who knew only her name from the headlines. Her name. Not Jaren's. Not his father's. Hers.

Taylor stood at the podium, a microphone pinned discreetly to her blouse. She scanned the room. Rows of young faces, notebooks open, pens ready.

She didn't need notes.

"I wasn't supposed to matter," she began. "I was quiet. I didn't fit. I wore secondhand shoes and read books most people hadn't heard of. I wasn't anyone's idea of a revolution."

She paused.

"But the truth is, change doesn't ask for permission. It doesn't arrive dressed like power. It arrives wearing humility. It arrives asking questions no one wants to answer. And it begins, not in boardrooms or newsrooms, but in quiet hearts that decide enough is enough."

Students leaned forward. She told them about the café, the foam, the gold-dust lies. She told them about her father's voice, the weight of silence, the day she opened the door and found her voice waiting.

And then she read.

From her journal.

She read the letter from the miner's sister. She read the line she had written the night her key disappeared.

"I am not the girl in the hallway anymore. I am the voice at the end of the corridor. I am the reckoning."

When she finished, there was no applause. Just stillness.

Then a single student stood. A young woman with braids and a trembling lip. "Thank you," she said. "For telling the truth."

Taylor smiled. "Thank you for hearing it."

Later, Taylor wandered back through her old neighborhood. The trees lining the streets were taller than she remembered. The brick buildings less imposing. She passed the library where she had spent her childhood afternoons, and the bench where she had once cried quietly after school, hiding her face from the world.

She stopped there.

Sat down.

Let herself feel everything.

A woman passed with a stroller and smiled.

"Nice day," she said.

Taylor nodded. "Yes. It really is."

The wind brushed through her hair, and she lifted her face to it.

She remembered Jaren's laughter. The good parts. The way he had looked at her sometimes, as if he saw her. The hope she had allowed to take root.

She remembered the betrayal. The silence. The apology too late to matter.

And she forgave him.

Not aloud. Not with words.

But with breath.

With the simple act of continuing.

That evening, Taylor met Mrs. Best for dinner in a quiet French restaurant tucked beneath ivy-covered walls.

The older woman raised a glass. "To the beginning."

Taylor clinked hers gently. "To the becoming."

They ate slowly, talked about the future of the Best foundation, now being restructured to fund schools and ethical mining oversight. Mrs. Best shared that she had begun mentoring young women who had once been ignored in boardrooms.

"I tell them about you," she said.

Taylor blinked. "About me?"

"Yes. I say, 'There was once a woman who walked into a lion's den without armor, and when they tried to devour her, she showed them what grace looks like with teeth.'"

Taylor laughed softly, tears forming. "That sounds dramatic."

"It was," Mrs. Best said. "And it was true."

As the meal ended, Taylor pulled a folded piece of paper from her purse. "I've been writing again. Not just in my journal."

Mrs. Best's eyes lit. "A book?"

Taylor nodded. "I think it's time."

"What's the title?"

Taylor's voice was steady.

**"The Harder They Fall."**

The woman across from her beamed. "It's perfect."

And it was.

When Taylor walked home that night, the city shimmered around her. Every footstep felt like punctuation. Not an ending.

A continuation.

She reached her door, turned the key, and stepped into the home she had made. Her safe place. Her writing desk waited. The piano waited. The firelight curled gently in the grate.

She sat.

And wrote.

For herself.

For her father.

For every girl who had ever swallowed her voice.

And as the final line took shape, she knew:

This wasn't the end of her story.

It was the beginning of everyone else's.

## Chapter 17: Sleeping with Serpents

The quiet that followed the storm was deceptive. Taylor knew better than to trust it.

Two weeks had passed since the first exposé of the Best empire went public. The initial shockwaves had rippled far and wide, resignations, subpoenas, headlines screaming truths once buried beneath designer suits and polished lies. But Taylor also understood something more insidious.

There were those who did not panic.

They waited.

And it was the waiting that haunted her now.

That morning, she stood on her balcony, overlooking a city that never truly slept. She sipped her tea slowly, her breath forming soft clouds in the crisp air. Her fingers trembled just slightly around the porcelain.

A package had arrived on her doorstep. No return address. Just her name.

Inside, she found a photograph.

It was of her. Sitting on the bench outside her childhood library. Taken days ago.

No note. Just the image. A message without words.

Taylor held it now, the edges damp from her grip. Her mind raced but her exterior remained still. Whoever had sent it wanted fear. They wanted her to retreat, to vanish back into the shadows she had fought so hard to leave behind.

Instead, she made a call.

"I need to see you," she said.

That evening, she met Isabel Marchand in the basement of a historic hotel that had long ago been converted into a private wine bar. The lighting was low, the patrons discreet. Isabel was already seated, a tablet open in front of her.

"I've traced it," she said as Taylor slid into the booth. "The photo came from a surveillance contractor in Prague. One tied to an old investor in the Best network. Quiet money. Dangerous history."

Taylor nodded. "So, they're watching."

"They're waiting," Isabel said. "Waiting for you to make a mistake. Waiting for you to relax."

Taylor looked at her. "Then I won't."

Isabel narrowed her eyes. "You shouldn't be alone right now."

"I'm not."

She reached into her bag and pulled out a flash drive.

"This has everything. The next five chapters. Documents, testimonies, legal filings. If anything happens to me, I want you to send it everywhere. Not just to the journalist. To the people who won't be silenced."

Isabel took the drive. "And you?"

Taylor smiled faintly. "I'll be fine. I've slept beside serpents before."

The next morning, Taylor returned to the café. Her café. The one where her voice had first begun to shape itself, not as defense, but as declaration.

She ordered her usual.

The barista smiled. "Cappuccino masterpiece?"

Taylor laughed. "Of course. Let's see if the angels are still sculpting foam."

She sat by the window and opened her journal. The page was blank, but her mind was not. She had begun dreaming again, not of the past, but of futures. Libraries filled with her words. Classrooms where girls read her name and knew it meant more than survival.

As she wrote, a shadow moved in the reflection of the glass.

She looked up.

Jaren.

He wore no suit today. Just a coat, his hands in his pockets, his eyes tired.

"May I?" he asked.

She nodded, cautiously.

He sat, and for a moment they were simply two people at a table, history between them like a pane of glass neither could shatter.

"I didn't send the photo," he said.

"I know."

"They're scared of you now."

"They should be."

Jaren nodded. "I came to tell you… he's going to disappear."

"Your father?"

"He's preparing to leave the country. Transferring assets. Planning a way out."

Taylor set her pen down. "Then we stop him."

Jaren's voice softened. "He's still my father."

"And I'm still the daughter of a man your family helped destroy."

He swallowed hard. "I know."

Taylor leaned in. "You have a choice, Jaren. Be his legacy or break the chain."

His eyes met hers, filled with something fragile. "I want to be better."

"Then prove it."

Later that night, Taylor met Mrs. Best in her office. The room was quiet, the shelves lined with law books and portraits of a life lived both publicly and privately.

"He's running," Taylor said.

Mrs. Best didn't flinch. "We anticipated this."

"Jaren wants to help."

Mrs. Best looked down, then back up. "He still believes redemption is a matter of time."

Taylor's voice was steady. "I believe it's a matter of courage."

They outlined a plan. With Jaren's inside knowledge, they could intercept wire transfers, alert authorities, seize documentation. It would take days. Maybe weeks.

But they would not let him vanish.

By the time Taylor returned home, exhaustion clung to her like fog. She collapsed onto the couch and stared at the ceiling.

And then the knock came.

Sharp. Rhythmic.

She opened the door to find a small envelope taped to it. No sender. Again.

Inside, a single word: "Enough."

Taylor closed her eyes.

But she did not tremble.

She went to her piano. Opened the lid. Played a single note.

Then another.

The melody built slowly, rising from pain and fury and grace. It filled the room, and with each note, she whispered to herself.

"Not yet."

Outside, the serpents waited.

But inside, the reckoning was already awake.

She would not sleep.

She would not retreat.

She would stand.

And soon, the world would hear her roar.

---

## Chapter 18: Lockpicks and Lineage

The hallway was colder than she remembered.

Taylor stood just outside the door of the office that had once been forbidden to her, the place where secrets slept behind mahogany panels and ancestral pride. Her breath caught in her throat as she reached into her coat pocket and drew out a small leather pouch.

Inside were three tools.

Not weapons. Not files.

Lockpicks.

A gift from her late uncle, her father's brother, who had taught her as a child how to open what was meant to stay closed. She remembered sitting on a worn carpet in his garage, surrounded by padlocks and soda cans, his voice patient as he said, "Sometimes the things that are locked are hiding truths. If you ever need to find one, use your hands and your head."

Her uncle had disappeared during a civil investigation tied to mining safety. He never came home. Her father never forgave the silence surrounding it. Taylor now understood. The silence had been orchestrated.

She knelt before the locked cabinet in the study, the last one unopened, hidden behind a sliding panel Jaren had shown her on a sketched blueprint only days ago. It was the last chamber. The last veil.

The pick slid in with ease, then a second tool to torque the pins.

Click.

The lock surrendered.

Inside were ledgers unlike the others. Not financials. But names. Personal profiles. Reports on families, journalists, educators, officials. A map of manipulation. A legacy of control.

She found her father's name.

And her uncle's.

She sank back onto the floor, the papers spread around her like broken wings. Her hands trembled, and for the first time in weeks, she let herself cry.

Her father had written letters to the Best Foundation, years ago, exposing unsafe practices in the supply chain. He had begged them to intervene. Instead, they had buried his voice.

Her uncle had disappeared because he tried to investigate further. His name was tagged as "noncompliant."

The Bests had erased their names with the same hand they used to sign donation checks.

Taylor's sobs were silent, her breath short. But in the grief, there was fire.

She gathered the files, scanned them, and uploaded them to a secure drive. She made copies. Three. One for the authorities. One for the press.

And one for herself.

As she left the estate, Jaren stood by the gate.

He had been waiting.

She didn't slow her pace.

"Taylor," he said.

She stopped only a few feet away, the wind catching her coat like a banner.

"I know what you found," he said.

"Then you know why I'm done with silence."

He nodded. "I wanted to tell you. About your father. About what they did. I wanted to protect you."

"No," she said, her voice sharp. "You wanted to protect yourself."

Jaren stepped closer. "Please. I know there's no excuse. But let me help now. Let me testify. Let me destroy the machine from within."

Taylor looked into his eyes, searching for sincerity.

"Then do it. But not for me. For them."

She handed him a single sheet. Her father's last letter.

"Read that and ask yourself if you're ready to be the kind of man who deserves to be remembered differently."

She walked away.

He did not follow.

Later that night, Taylor sat with Mrs. Best in a quiet garden behind the restructured foundation's new offices. The air smelled of rosemary and hope.

"I read the files," Mrs. Best said. "All of them."

Taylor looked at her. "And?"

Mrs. Best's voice cracked. "I believed I was too far from it. I believed the sins were not mine. But I was wrong."

"We're all part of what we don't stop," Taylor whispered.

Mrs. Best nodded. "What will you do next?"

Taylor took a breath. "I'll go public. With my name. With the story."

"Are you sure?"

"Yes. They need to see a face. They need to see who they tried to erase."

Mrs. Best reached across the table and took her hand. "Then I will stand with you."

The press conference was scheduled for Thursday. It would be streamed live. Taylor rehearsed her statement only once.

She did not memorize.

She remembered.

On the day of the conference, Taylor wore a soft gray suit and her mother's pendant. Her hair was pulled back, and in her hand, she carried her father's final letter.

As she stood before the cameras, she spoke not as a victim, but as a witness.

She told them of a man who had believed in the power of words.

She told them of a girl who had been invisible, until she wrote herself into permanence.

She told them of ledgers and lies, of love and loss.

And when she finished, she read aloud the final line from her father's letter:

"Truth is not what we say when we are safe. Truth is what we say when we are scared, and say it anyway."

The room was still.

Then came the flood of questions.

She answered them all.

When she walked out into the light, the sun broke through the clouds.

That evening, she returned to the bench outside the library. A little girl sat there now, reading. Alone. Taylor smiled and sat beside her.

"What are you reading?" she asked.

The girl held up a book.

Taylor's name was on the cover.

The girl looked at her, wide-eyed and nervous. "You're Ms. Wilson. You're her. I mean, you're…"

Taylor nodded. "Yes. But so are you."

And in that moment, the world turned quietly.

Not loudly. Not with applause.

But with promise.

The kind that can only come after pain.

And is therefore unbreakable.

---

**Chapter 19: The Silent Stake**

The air in the boardroom was heavy with varnish and legacy. Deep mahogany walls reflected dim light from crystal sconces, casting on portraits that lined the space. The men in the paintings looked down as if disapproving of interruption, of any story that did not include their names.

Taylor stood at the head of the long table, the only woman in the room. Her palms rested lightly on the dark wood surface. Before her were copies of the final legal findings. And beside them, a silver fountain pen. Uncapped. Waiting for her grasp.

Across from her sat members of the Best Foundation's board. Some were financial magnates, others were former politicians, and a few legacy heirs had coasted on inherited privilege. All of them had known, in some form, the power behind the empire's polite façade. And each had looked the other way.

Not today.

Mrs. Best sat to Taylor's right, her hands folded neatly. She wore navy, her hair pinned with elegant precision. Her presence was calm. Her silence had weight.

Taylor inhaled slowly. Then began.

"This isn't just about the numbers. This isn't about balance sheets or optics. This is about children buried in unmarked graves, about fathers who vanished under false reports. About women paid in silence."

A man with silver hair and a tight jaw leaned forward. "You're asking us to sign away centuries of protection."

"I'm not asking," Taylor replied. "I'm showing you what the cost of silence has been. And I'm offering you a way to be remembered differently."

Another board member, younger, cleared his throat. "We've seen the press. We've read the files. But you need to understand what you're stepping into. These decisions echo."

Taylor met his eyes. "Good. Because so does accountability."

She gestured to the folder in front of her.

"This outlines a full divestment plan. All ties to shell corporations will be severed. All humanitarian efforts moving forward will be transparent, with third-party oversight. And the family name will no longer serve as a seal of exemption."

The room fell deathly quiet.

Mrs. Best finally spoke.

"I have reviewed the documents. I support them fully. If you do not, I will resign and take my shares public. And the world will know that even when you were handed the truth, you chose comfort over courage."

The older man stared at her. "You would do that?"

"I have nothing left to protect except the women like Taylor who walked through this fire without armor."

Taylor said nothing. She did not need to. Mrs. Best had just cast her vote with thunder.

The board began to sign.

One by one.

The final signature came from the youngest member. He looked at Taylor and nodded slightly, a flicker of respect in his eyes.

It was done.

When the room cleared, Mrs. Best reached for Taylor's hand.

"You didn't just hold the line," she said. "You redrew it."

Outside, the city glimmered. But Taylor did not return home.

She went to a quiet cemetery at the edge of town. The sky was soft with early evening. Clouds hovered like gentle watchers. She carried a single envelope.

She approached slowly to her father's grave. A simple stone. No grand epitaph. Just his name, and the word "teacher."

She knelt and placed the envelope beside the marker.

"I did it, Dad," she whispered. "I told the truth. And they listened."

Tears came, but they did not fall. They stayed in her eyes like light.

She sat there for a long while.

Not speaking. Just being.

As she rose to leave, she felt the wind. It carried the scent of flowers. Jasmine, perhaps. Her mother's favorite.

When Taylor returned to her apartment, the light on her answering machine blinked.

She pressed play.

"Miss Wilson," a voice said, one she did not recognize. "This is with the United Nations panel. We've reviewed your documents. We would like to invite you to speak in Geneva. Full arrangements will be made. You've started something we believe in."

Taylor stood still, the machine blinking again as the message ended.

Another began.

"Taylor. It's me."

Jaren.

"I know I'm the last voice you want to hear. But I need you to know. I testified. I named names. I gave them everything. Not for redemption. Just because it's the only thing I've ever done without asking what I'd get in return."

A pause.

"I won't ask for anything. Not even forgiveness. I just wanted you to know. You changed me. And that change matters."

She deleted the message.

Not out of anger. But because she did not need it.

She reached for her pen.

And began writing.

Not in her journal.

In her manuscript.

**The Harder They Fall.**

The chapter title? "The Silent Stake."

She wrote of every boardroom, every closed door, every locked cabinet, and shattered illusion. She wrote of her father's letters, of her uncle's silence, of her own voice rising in the stillness.

She wrote the names of those who had tried to stop her.

And those who had stood beside her.

She paused only once.

To whisper thanks.

To remember.

Just before her eyes began to tire, Taylor's manuscript was almost finished.

She sent it to her publisher with a single line note:

"For the girls who keep getting up."

She sat back, the weight of years finally lifting.

And in that moment, she understood something her father had once said.

"The world may not clap for you, but if you stand long enough in truth, it will shift around you."

And it had.

She had not won with power.

She had won with presence.

The silent stake had always been hers.

She just had to claim it.

**Chapter 20: The Gentle Revolution**

There are revolutions that begin with fire.

And then there are the ones that begin with a whisper.

Taylor sat beneath the skylight of the Best Foundation's newly transformed offices, her journal open across her lap, her pen poised above a page titled simply: "What Comes Next." The world around her had tilted and shifted in the months since she revealed the truth, and now it was her task to help rebuild what had been hollowed by greed and pompous lies.

But this chapter, she knew, required a different kind of strength. Not the thunder of defiance, but the quiet resolve of repair.

The sun spilled over the room's restored oak floors, once lacquered in polish and distance, now warm and worn like something finally human. In the corner, volunteers were arranging binders filled with new program outlines, grants for ethical mining initiatives, scholarships for displaced youth, and a legal aid clinic dedicated to whistleblowers across industries.

This was the revolution Taylor had always believed in.

Soft-footed. Clear-eyed. Relentless.

Mrs. Best entered quietly, carrying a box marked "Archives." She set it down on the table beside Taylor with a tired smile.

"I found these in storage," she said. "Letters from early beneficiaries. Before everything turned."

Taylor opened the box and pulled out one envelope. Inside was a note scrawled in pencil, likely from a child: "Thank you for the shoes. I'm going to school now. My sister says I walk taller."

Taylor folded the letter with trembling fingers.

"They were better before. What changed?" Mrs. Best said, her voice soft. "Once. Before the money changed their hearts."

Taylor looked at her. "Then let's change it back."

Later that day, she stood before a class of students at a women's center in Brooklyn. The room was filled with young women of different backgrounds, different languages, but all with the same look in their eyes: hunger. Not for approval. For possibility.

Taylor shared her story. The girl in the hallway. The woman in the boardroom. The moment her voice became louder than her fear.

**And then, she asked them to write.**

**"Write to the version of you that almost gave up," she said. "Tell her what she became."**

She walked among them as pens scratched paper, as tears fell.

One girl stood to read.

"I thought I was broken," she began. "But I was just bending toward the light."

Taylor wept, but with a smile, and so did the room.

Afterward, one of the center's counselors pulled her aside.

"We've never seen them be so open," she said. "They trust you."

"They don't trust me," Taylor replied. "They see now what they can be."

That evening, Taylor returned home to find an envelope slid beneath her door. This time, it was from Isabel.

Inside was a copy of a newly signed treaty, an international agreement for fair trade certification of raw materials. Taylor's name was listed in the preamble, credited for "awakening global conscience."

She pressed the paper to her chest.

And for the second time today, she wept.

Not from sorrow.

From astonishment.

That her voice, once too small to echo down a school hallway, now shaped change.

The following week, Taylor stood at the foot of a stage in Geneva. The UN session had concluded. Her testimony had been received, her words translated into six languages. She had spoken of transparency, of moral courage, of the courage it takes to dismantle a structure built in silence.

When she descended the podium, applause followed her. But it was not for her eloquence.

It was for her endurance.

In a private reception afterward, a diplomat approached her.

"My daughter read your book," he said. "She now wants to study journalism. She says she wants to be brave the way you are."

Taylor's voice caught. "Tell her she already is. She just needs to keep believing in herself."

He nodded. "You've done more than change policy. You've changed imagination."

On her return flight, Taylor stared out the window at the clouds. They looked like land not yet walked on. She opened her journal and began a new section: "The Revolution We Cannot Measure."

She wrote of the girls who would never meet her, but who would walk through doors she had helped unlock.

She wrote of the women who had remained behind curtains, and the ones who had come forward.

And she wrote of Mrs. Best.

Not as a benefactor.

As a fellow survivor.

When she landed, a car waited. A bouquet of lilies on the seat. A note from Mrs. Best:

"Thank you for reminding us that revolution is not rage. It is remembrance."

Taylor closed her eyes.

That weekend, the foundation launched its first public campaign under new leadership. The tagline: "Truth, Told and Carried."

Taylor stood at the ribbon cutting with volunteers and former employees who had once feared speaking up. They smiled for photos. But the real moment came later, when a group of high school girls arrived for a mentoring session.

Taylor leaned forward.

"What do you want to build?" she asked.

One girl answered without hesitation. "A world where no one asks that question, because they already believe we can."

Taylor reached for the young girl's hand.

And knew.

The change had begun.

Not with fire.

With faith.

The kind born from surviving.

From enduring.

From becoming.

---

## Chapter 21: Cappuccino Queen

The air in the café was sweetened with nostalgia.

Taylor stepped over the threshold and paused. It had been months since she'd last stood here, but it might as well have been years. The café looked the same, down to the gold-framed menu board, the velvet armchairs near the window, and the chandelier that sparkled like conversation in glass. But something was different. The baristas looked up with recognition, not curiosity.

She walked to the counter, a soft murmur spreading through the quiet crowd.

"Welcome back, Miss Wilson," said the young woman behind the register, her voice touched with reverence. "Your usual?"

Taylor smiled. "Let's make it official."

She cleared her throat and began her soliloquy, *"I would like a cappuccino masterpiece. Not merely a drink, but a hymn in foam. Whispered from the soul of an espresso bean, coaxed into glory by milk warmed in a promise. And may the top be graced with something divine, as if angels stirred it with their wings."*

The room, once hushed, broke into a soft wave of laughter and applause. She turned to face them, surprised to see cameras, phones discreetly capturing the moment. Not for spectacle. For memory.

A young woman approached her.

"I came all the way from Baltimore," she said. "I read your book three times. My little sister can't stop saying she wants to be a 'cappuccino queen' just like you."

Taylor felt a bit overwhelmed.

"Then she already is," she replied. "Because she sees herself."

The cappuccino arrived, its foam crowned with a silhouette of her profile in cocoa dust. She laughed, touched but humbled.

She took her seat by the window.

And watched.

Students gathered at corner tables, whispering lines from her testimony. A mother sat with her daughter, reading from a magazine that featured Taylor on the cover. The girl pointed and smiled.

Taylor sipped her cappuccino slowly, letting the warmth settle her. Not from the drink. From the belonging.

This was where it had all begun. The tiny rebellions. The whispered confidence. The first time she had ordered something in a voice that did not tremble.

And now the world recognized she was not invisible.

A few minutes later, a familiar face appeared at the door.

It was Elijah, her high school librarian. Older now, but with the same thoughtful eyes.

"May I join you?" he asked.

"Please," she said, rising to embrace him.

"I wanted to see the girl who changed the world," he said, as he settled across from her.

"I didn't change it," Taylor replied. "I just offered a reminder."

He nodded. "Of what?"

"That stillness can be strength. That softness is not surrender. That truth is its own kind of armor."

He looked down at the book on the table. **The Harder They Fall.**

"I kept your old essays," he said. "The ones you submitted late because you were too nervous to share. I read them again last week. The fire was always there."

She smiled through tears. "You were the first person who ever wrote the word 'powerful' on anything I created."

"Because you are," he said.

They talked for over an hour. About books, about memory, about how sometimes the smallest moments become the turning points. And when he left, he softly pressed his face to her ear and whispered, "I never doubted you."

Taylor sat there, overwhelmed and grounded all at once.

That evening, she was scheduled to appear at a university gala in honor of emerging female leaders. She had nearly declined. But something in her spirit had said yes.

She arrived dressed in navy, the color of resilience. Her speech was not long.

"I didn't come here to speak about success," she told them. "I came to speak about beginnings. About the girl in the hallway. The woman with shaking hands. The moment you think you've been forgotten, only to realize you've been remembering yourself."

The room applauded. But more than that, they leaned forward. Not toward fame.

Toward faith.

After the event, a journalist caught up to her.

"One last question," he said. "What's next for Taylor Wilson?"

She paused.

"I'm writing again. But not alone. I've launched a fellowship. Women from every walk of life will gather to tell their stories. Unfiltered. Unedited. Just as they are."

He scribbled something in his notebook, then looked up. "And what will it be called?"

Taylor thought of the café. Of the gold foam. Of the girl she had been and the queen she had become.

"Cappuccino Queens," she said.

And then she turned and walked away.

After arriving home, she opened a letter that had been waiting for her.

It was from Jaren.

No apologies. Just truth.

"Thank you for being who I could not. Thank you for becoming what I never had the courage to be. I've started over. I am working with survivors now. I'm learning, every day, what it means to listen."

Taylor placed the letter in her journal. No tears. Just grace.

She sat at her desk, surrounded by letters from girls across the world.

And she wrote one back.

To the girl in the hallway.

**"Dear You,**

**You are not small. You are not invisible. You are the beginning of every brave thing I ever became.**

**Keep walking.**

**Love,**

**Me."**

Outside, the city moved with its usual tempo.

But in that moment, Taylor heard something more.

Not applause.

A heartbeat.

Her own.

Steady.

True.

A crown not worn but lived.

She was the cappuccino queen.

And she was just getting started.

---

## Chapter 22: Letters Never Sent

Taylor always kept a box beneath her bed. Not for valuables, not for hidden cash or lost keepsakes. This one held something softer. Something heavier. Letters.

She pulled it out one early morning, just as the first light of day touched the window. The world outside was quiet, and in the hush of dawn, there was something sacred in returning to the places we kept our truths. She opened the lid.

Inside were envelopes, some sealed, others opened and re-read so many times the creases had begun to fray. She ran her fingers over each one, as if greeting old friends or forgotten ghosts. These were the letters she had written but never sent.

To her father. To Jaren. To the girl in the hallway. To herself.

She laid them out across the bed like pages in an unfinished book.

The first was dated years ago.

**Dear Dad,**

*I don't know how to carry your silence. Sometimes I pretend I hear you in the sound of the wind. Other days, I forget your voice and shed tears because it feels like betrayal. I'm trying to be brave, but bravery feels a lot like pretending. If you were here, would you still call me*

*Taybird? Would you tell me I matter, even when the world seems not to notice?*

*I miss the way you listened. You made everything feel possible. I promise I'll keep listening. Even when it's hard.*

*Love,*

*Taylor*

She closed her eyes, remembering the scent of his sweater, the candor of his laughter. He had been her first safe place. And even now, years later, he remained her reason.

The next letter was written after the first time Jaren failed to defend her.

**Dear Jaren,**

*You watched them mock me, and you smiled. You called it teasing, but it felt like betrayal. I wanted you to intervene, protect me. Anything. I would have settled for a glance that told them this was wrong, that I wasn't invisible.*

*Instead, you were still. Silent. Polished. And I learned, in that moment, that some betrayals don't come with knives. Some come with silence.*

She never showed him that one. But in writing it, she had found her own voice again.

Another letter was to a girl she had once passed on the subway. A girl, maybe thirteen, reading a poetry book with torn corners.

**Dear You,**

*I saw you. On the D line. Your coat was too big and your shoes had holes, but your eyes... your eyes were brilliant. You read like you were saving yourself. I wanted to tell you then, you don't need to shrink to survive. There's room for you in this world, even if it tries to tell you otherwise.*

*Keep reading. Keep writing. You're the author now of your story. Take a bow.*

*Love,*

*Someone who once sat where you are.*

A tear of joy arose from that memory. That girl had reminded her who she'd been.

Then there was the hardest one.

**Dear Me,**

*You were not weak for crying. You were not naive for hoping. You were not a fool for loving him. You gave your heart without an invoice. That is not a flaw. That is courage.*

*When they called you too quiet, too soft, too sensitive, they were trying to name what they feared. Your gentleness was not a deficiency. It was resilients.*

*You survived. Not because you fought back with fists, but because you stayed. Because you kept writing. Because you kept believing.*

*I am so proud of you.*

*Love,*

*Your future*

Taylor folded that one gently and placed it on top.

She carried the box to her writing desk and began transcribing parts of the letters into a new manuscript. This one wasn't about exposure or justice. It was about healing.

She titled it: **Letters Never Sent.**

It would be a collection. Part memoir, part meditation. All heart.

She wrote all morning.

By noon, the scent of coffee drifted through the air. She stood, stretching, and wandered to her kitchen. The city moved gently beyond her windows. She turned on soft music and let the piano notes fill the space.

Her phone buzzed.

A message from Isabel: "The girls in Nairobi got their first shipment of books. They were overjoyed. All signed copies of your novel." Taylor paused and smiled inside.

Later that day, she visited a youth center in Harlem. She sat in a circle with teens who had all survived something: loss, violence, abandonment. One by one, they read letters they had written to someone they'd never gotten to forgive.

A boy read to his friends, lost.

A girl read to her future child.

And then they asked Taylor to read something.

She chose the letter to her younger self.

By the end, there wasn't a dry eye in the room.

One girl stood to embrace her. "Thank you for giving us the words."

"You've had them all along," Taylor said.

That evening, she returned home and opened the last letter.

It wasn't one she had written.

It had arrived anonymously weeks ago. She had tucked it away, unsure if she was ready.

She read it now.

**Dear Taylor,**

*I watched you speak on the steps of the courthouse. You looked like a lighthouse. I realized I'd spent my life pretending the storm wasn't real. You never once claimed to be perfect. But you were honest. That's rarer than virtue.*

*I'm sorry I didn't protect you. I'm sorry I let them question your light. If I could do it again, I would stand beside you, not behind you.*

*You deserve everything. Every peace. Every joy. Every crown.*

*Your voice saved me.*

Love,

J.

She closed the letter.

And wept.

Not because it changed anything.

Because it mattered.

That night, she boxed the letters and tied the lid with a ribbon.

Then she wrote one final note.

**Dear Reader,**

*You are not alone. Whatever silence you've carried, whatever words you haven't spoken, know this, your story is waiting to be told. Not perfectly. Just truthfully. That is enough.*

Love,

*Taylor*

She sealed the envelope.

And slipped it between the pages of the final draft.

The story was hers.

And it was theirs.

A legacy not in ink.

But in letters never sent.

And now, finally, received.

---

## Chapter 23: The Weight of Yes

Taylor stood at the edge of the stage, the microphone just inches away. A single spotlight carved her silhouette into the dark velvet backdrop, illuminating her presence but not yet her voice. Rows of seats stretched before her, filled with faces upturned in hope, curiosity, and the sacred hush that precedes something unforgettable.

This was the Literary Freedom Summit, a global gathering of thinkers, poets, storytellers, and survivors. And Taylor had been named the keynote.

She hadn't planned on saying yes.

The invitation had come weeks ago, slipped between letters of gratitude and publisher offers. At first, she had laughed. Then she had wept. And finally, she had stared at the word "decline" on her email screen until it blurred.

It wasn't fear that made her hesitate.

It was the weight.

Because a yes, she knew, was never just a word.

It was a door.

She stepped toward the mic.

"Before I speak, I want to tell you a story," she began. "Not the one you've read. Not the one you've seen online. A quieter one."

The room stilled.

"There was a little girl who never raised her hand in class. Not once. She knew the answer. She always knew. But silence felt safer. Safer than being wrong. Safer than being mocked."

Taylor paused.

"I was that girl. But more than that, I became the woman who built her life around avoiding the spotlight. Around surviving, not thriving."

A shift rippled through the audience, gentle but meaningful.

"And then one day, someone said my name. Not to dismiss me. Not to command me. Just to acknowledge me. And it was as if I'd been given permission to exist."

She took a breath.

"I wrote that name down. Not theirs. Mine. Because if someone else could say it with respect, I could learn to say it with love."

A murmur of emotion swept through the room.

Taylor's voice softened.

"And now, here I am. Standing not because I am the bravest. But because I finally said yes. Not to fame or fortune. Not to a book deal. But to myself."

She closed her eyes for a moment, then opened them slowly. Embracing the moment.

"We talk about the power of no. And yes, no is powerful. It builds boundaries. It protects. But so is yes. Yes, is how we open. Yes, is how we reclaim. Yes, is how we begin again."

Her fingers gripped the sides of the podium.

"My father used to say, 'A whisper of truth is louder than a roar of fiction.' And so today, I whisper to every girl who has ever thought her voice too soft, her fear too loud, her dreams too fragile."

She leaned forward.

"Say yes to the voice inside you that won't stay quiet. Say yes to your rage, your grace, your questions. Say yes to becoming."

The applause was not immediate.

It was appreciation.

And when it came, it grew like a rising tide. Not performative. Not polite.

Powerful.

Taylor stepped away from the podium, resting her hand on her heart, and left the stage. Embracing the audience of survivors all at once in that moment.

Backstage, she found a small envelope on the dressing table. No name. Just a wax seal in the shape of a feather.

Inside, a note:

"Your yes gave birth to mine. Keep going. We are following in your footsteps."

She folded the note gently, placed it in her journal, and pressed her fingers to her heart.

That night, she walked alone through a park near the summit hall. The path curved beneath lanterns strung between trees, casting golden light on the leaves. She sat on a bench beneath a chestnut tree as the cool air kissed her cheek.

A child passed on a bicycle. A couple whispered dreams to each other. A woman, walking alone, nodded at her.

And Taylor thought: this is what yes becomes.

Not fame.

But freedom.

When she returned to her hotel, she opened her laptop and began writing her next book. It wouldn't be about justice this time. Or reckoning.

It would be about joy.

About what happens after the tears.

About the dance that comes when you realize you've survived.

She titled the first page: "The Weight of Yes."

And beneath it, she wrote:

"I once carried my silence like a shield. Now I wear my yes like a crown."

And she smiled.

Not because it was done.

Because it had begun.

---

## Chapter 24: Her Name Was Taylor

The bookstore was small. Tucked between a flower shop and a record store on a quiet corner of Brooklyn, it didn't boast neon lights or grand window displays. Just shelves worn with love, and the gentle hush of pages breathing.

Taylor stood at the entrance for a moment, her hand resting on the frame. Inside, voices rose in excited tones. It was her final tour stop. The end of a long, winding journey. And she had chosen this place not for the size of the crowd, but for the weight of memory.

Her first book signing had taken place here. Three years ago. Seven people had come.

Today, there were more than seventy.

She stepped inside and was greeted with applause. Not thunderous. But warm.

Humbling.

A little girl, no older than nine, handed her a crayon drawing. It was a picture of a girl standing tall with a book in one hand and a glowing heart in the other. Beneath it, in big letters, the girl had written: "Her name was Taylor."

Taylor smiled and moved close enough to whisper.

"Is this me?"

The girl innocently nodded.

Taylor offered her a hug, and the little girl fell forward like falling into a pillow. "It's beautiful. Thank you."

She took her seat at the signing table and began writing notes in the books handed to her.

"For the ones still whispering."

"For the girls finding their voice."

"For the quiet power within you."

As the line moved, faces passed like a tide. A teacher. A nurse. A survivor of domestic abuse who said Taylor's words helped her leave. A man who cried as he said he had never heard a voice like hers before.

Each one left something behind. A piece of their own story, woven into the fabric of hers.

After the last book was signed, the bookstore owner pulled Taylor aside.

"There's someone in the back," she said. "Didn't want to stand in line. Just wanted a moment."

Taylor nodded and walked through the rows of books until she reached the back table. A woman stood there, facing the window. Her coat hung neatly on the chair beside her.

When she turned, Taylor stopped.

It was her mother.

They hadn't spoken in nearly a year. Not from anger. From space.

"I didn't know you were coming," Taylor said, her voice soft.

"I had to come," her mother replied. "It was intimidating when I saw the crowd outside. But then, I saw the sign with your name. And I remembered all the nights you stayed up writing. I remembered you reading to yourself out loud because no one else would listen."

Taylor's heart became full of emotions.

"I wanted to tell you something," her mother continued.

Taylor waited.

"I'm proud of you. Not just because they are. Because I see who you are. Who you've become. And I think your father would have said it better, but I'll say it anyway. You made this world better, just by being true to yourself."

Tears filled Taylor's eyes.

"Thank you, mother." She whispered.

They embraced.

Longer than they ever had before.

When her mother left, Taylor sat at the back table and opened her journal.

She began writing the epilogue to her next book.

"Her name was Taylor. She did not arrive with a crown. She arrived with questions. With tremors in her voice. With journals filled with dreams. And when they ignored her, she wrote louder. When they silenced her, she stood taller. When they tried to unwrite her, she pressed pen to paper and made herself permanent."

"She was not perfect. She was not finished. But she was here, unbothered, and apologetic."

Taylor paused, then wrote one last line.

"And that, in the end, was more than enough."

As she stood to leave, the bookstore owner handed her a small wrapped package.

"Someone left this for you. No name."

Inside was a leather-bound notebook.

On the first page, in handwriting she didn't recognize, were the words:

"For the next Taylor."

She smiled.

Closed the book.

And walked into the evening light, her heart steady, her voice ready.

The girl in the hallway was gone.

And in her place stood a woman who answered to her own name.

Taylor.

---

**Epilogue**

The sun was setting over the Hudson, its reflection stretching in golden ribbons across the water. Taylor stood at the edge of the foundation's rooftop garden, a mug of tea in hand. The city moved below her, not hurried or loud, but present.

It had been exactly one year since the release of her first book. Twelve months since her name became more than a whisper in backrooms or a footnote in someone else's narrative. The world had read her story. But more importantly, it had listened.

She had changed the laws in three countries. Spoken at seventeen institutions. Launched a global initiative for ethical sourcing. But when asked what mattered most, she always said the same thing.

"The letters."

Because each day, new ones came.

From girls who had found their voice.

From women who had left what they once believed they couldn't.

From men who had begun unlearning.

Tonight, she would read them all.

But first, she walked back inside, where a small group of writers sat waiting. They were part of her fellowship. The very first cohort. Eight women. Eight stories. Each of them raw, radiant, still becoming.

Taylor sat among them.

"We write," she said, "not to escape the truth. But to shape it, reveal it."

They nodded.

"And when we speak," she continued, "we do so not to impress. But to remember. Who we are. Who we were. Who we're still becoming."

They picked up their pens all at once in solidarity.

And as the room filled with the soft sound of ink on paper, Taylor turned to the first page of her next journal.

She wrote:

*"I am not here because I was the loudest. I am here because I was the most willing to be heard."*

Then she closed her eyes.

And in the quiet that followed, she heard them.

All of them.

The girls who never raised their hand.

The women who stayed too long.

The voices once buried beneath boardrooms and boardwalks and backrooms and basements.

All saying the same thing.

We are here. We are here.

And she smiled.

Because she knew.

So was she.

No longer Taylor-Timid.

Just Taylor.

---

**The End**

www.ingramcontent.com/pod-product-compliance
Lightning Source LLC
LaVergne TN
LVHW042245070526
838201LV00088B/27